Helen Wright.

STUDY GUIDE
TO
EPHESIANS

by

FRANCIS FOULKES, M.A., B.D., M.SC.

Principal of the C.M.S. Federal Training Centre, Melbourne,
Australia, and formerly Principal of the Vining
Christian Leadership Centre, Akure, Nigeria

But now in ... ho once
were far off ... near
in the ble ... 3.

D1394583

INTER-VARSITY PRESS

INTER-VARSITY PRESS

Inter-Varsity Fellowship
39 *Bedford Square, London WC*1

Inter-Varsity Christian Fellowship
1**3**0 *north Wells, Chicago, Illinois* 60606

© F. FOULKES
First edition June 1968

U.K. STANDARD BOOK NUMBERS

85110 341 3 (Inter-Varsity Press)
85352 302 9 (Africa Christian Press)

Printed in Great Britain by
Billing & Sons Limited
Guildford and London

PREFACE

THE PURPOSE of these studies is a simple one. It is hoped that they will help those who read them to understand and apply to their lives more of the great riches of wisdom and knowledge that the Scriptures contain. Such short studies cannot hope to cover every detail of each verse. They make an attempt to consider the main points of teaching in a passage. Where there are things difficult to understand, the Notes at the bottom of the sections try to deal with them a little more fully. The purpose is not just that these studies should feed the mind with the knowledge of Scripture and its teaching. Each study ends with prayer, because the reading of the Bible should always lead us to the response of repentance and faith and obedience, and we express this first in prayer and then in action in our daily lives. The book has been divided up into passages that are not too long to be used for daily study and meditation, if so desired. For those who, as students of the Word, want to go more deeply and to compare scripture with scripture, the suggestions for further study are added.

The Revised Standard Version is the translation which has been used, because of the greater simplicity of its English, and because of the increasing use of this version in places where this book may be read.

TO THE EPHESIANS

To MANY people this is the greatest and best-loved of all Paul's letters. Certainly it is quite different from all the others. When we read 1 Corinthians or Galatians, we see immediately the problems the apostle had to deal with in the churches to which he wrote. When we read 2 Corinthians or Philippians, we realize how Paul's letters usually are full of personal references, greetings, and messages to particular individuals in the churches. In this letter there is no reference to special problems. Paul says little of himself except that as a prisoner for Christ's sake he was praying for and encouraging his readers (3:1; 4:1; 6:19–20). The only other person he mentions by name is Tychicus, the messenger who carried the letter (6:21–22).

The letter has one great aim, to show to all who read it the amazing purpose of God in His Son Jesus Christ, and how He is working out that purpose in His church. We may call the first half of the letter doctrinal, though that does not mean that it is a careful and ordered statement of Christian belief; Romans is the only letter where we find anything like that. In this letter doctrine is expressed in praise and prayer. In 1:3–14 the list of the blessings that men receive in Christ is full of doctrine, but it is in fact a hymn of praise. The apostle's words in 1:15–22 about the resurrection and exaltation of Christ and about His place as Head of the church are of great doctrinal importance, but they are words of prayer. In chapter 2 Paul sets out two great foundation truths: first, that men who were dead in sin are brought to new life in Christ, and so they come to have part in the great purpose of God; and secondly, that those who have been enemies are brought to peace and unity by the reconciliation that Christ has made possible. Then, after speaking of his great privilege in being called to preach to the Gentiles 'the unsearchable riches of Christ' (3:1–13), he goes on to pray that his readers may know the full measure of the love of Christ indwelling them (3:14–21). Then chapters 4–5 show the high calling and the great task of Christians in the light of this purpose of God. Paul has shown the way of peace and unity through Christ. Next he emphasizes the practical importance of that unity which Christians keep by realizing how much they have to share, and by an attitude of humility and longsuffering, and by realizing also the different gifts that the ascended Lord gives to each member for the building up of the whole of Christ's body (4:1–16). The nature of the new life that replaces the old is the subject of the next paragraph (4:17 – 5:2) – truth, honesty and love must replace falsehood and bitterness. Light has replaced darkness, and as children of light Christians must live in purity and God-given wisdom (5:3–21). Then Paul turns to relationships through which (as much as in the personal life) Christians must honour their Lord and show His ways in the world – wives and husbands, children and parents, servants and masters (5:22 – 6:9). The letter closes with the reminder that the Christian life is conflict against spiritual powers of evil, conflict in which Christ's warriors need the strength of God and the armour of God to stand firm and to win the battle (6:10–24).

Because this letter deals with no particular problems, we do not need to think specially of the background of the church or churches to which it was first written, as we do with Paul's other letters. Here, rather, we want

5

to study the words and expressions Paul uses; and the more we do so, the more deeply we will come to understand the purpose of God as Paul came to know it. So also we will come more truly to see the kind of life we should live, if we are to fulfil our part in that purpose, as members of the body of Christ.

Prayer. *Lord God Almighty, we praise Thee that we are not left in darkness, but in the Scriptures we have the light of the knowledge of Thee and of Thy purpose. Help us to open the doors of our hearts and minds to receive Thy truth. And, as we learn Thy way, may we have strength to obey Thy will, and to live in accordance with Thy high calling in Jesus Christ Thy Son, our Saviour.* AMEN.

ANALYSIS OF THE LETTER

Ephesians 1–3
THE PURPOSE OF GOD IN CHRIST

Ephesians 4–6
THE PURPOSE OF GOD IN THE CHRISTIAN

BOOKS RECOMMENDED

The following more detailed commentaries on Ephesians are recommended:

W. Barclay, *The Daily Study Bible*: *The Letters to the Galatians and Ephesians* (St. Andrew Press)

F. F. Bruce, *The Epistle to the Ephesians* (Pickering and Inglis)

F. Foulkes, *The Epistle of Paul to the Ephesians* (Tyndale New Testament Commentary, Tyndale Press)

H. C. G. Moule, *Ephesian Studies* (Pickering and Inglis)

1:1–2.   GREETING

LETTERS OF the time usually began with the name of the writer, the readers, a greeting, and then thanksgiving and prayer for the readers. Often these were expressed in a very formal way; but when Paul wrote, each one of these was full of Christian meaning.

Study 1. THE WRITER

'Paul, an apostle of Christ Jesus by the will of God' (1:1a).

Paul had a Jewish name, Saul; but from the time that he began his great missionary work among the Gentiles he took the Gentile name Paul (Acts 13:9, 13). This was the name he was known by in the story of his missionary work and in his letters. But the description of himself that we have here is what is most important.

a. He was an apostle

An apostle means simply one who is sent. Luke's

9

Gospel, from the time when the twelve were first sent out to work for the Lord, calls them no longer 'disciples' but 'apostles' (Luke 9:10). Paul sometimes used the word to speak of the authority of his position in the churches, as one sent by God, His special messenger. But he thought more often of the privilege than of the authority. Above all he thought of the life and work that it meant for him; everything depended on the fact that he was a man called and sent by God. He was not master of his own life, to choose his work, or to say what he would do each day. Once and for all, God had sent him. Therefore, daily and all the day, and to the end of his life, he was an apostle. This affected all his relationships with people, and all the ways that he used his time and strength.

b. He was an apostle by the will of God

Paul realized the honour and privilege of his position, and its responsibility, but he would always emphasize that he did not have it by right, nor by his own choice, and certainly not because he in any way deserved it. It was entirely by the will of God, and on this he relied when his apostleship was challenged, and doubtless in times of temptation too. Hebrews 5:4 says about the work of a priest in Old Testament days, that no-one could take the honour on himself, but he must be called by God. Paul felt exactly like this about his position as an apostle. He had been a persecutor, and he felt that he was 'the very least of all the saints' (3:8). He knew that it was not just because he had come to choose this way, but that God had chosen him (see John 15:16). He was an apostle, not by the decision or action of any man (Galatians 1:1), but because of the will of God which became clear to him in a blinding flash on the road to Damascus (Acts 9:3–6). From that day, no part of his life could ever be the same again.

There was a special position and work of an 'apostle' in the church in New Testament times (see on 4:11), and no-one can be an apostle today in quite the same way as those who had seen the risen Lord and been sent by Him. It is also true that not all Christians today are called to the 'full-time ministry' of the church. But every Christian is a person who is sent. All who have come to Christ in faith, willing to receive His mercy, willing to obey, are sent out to be His witnesses (Acts 1:8), and to live for Him in the world. For us, as for Paul, this fact should affect all our life, our friendships, our work, our use of talents and possessions.

Prayer. *Jesus, Lord and Master, we have not chosen to serve Thee, but Thou in Thy everlasting mercy hast put Thy hand on us. Help us every day to go out into the world, as sent by Thee, to do Thy will, to tell Thy gospel, to bring Thy blessing to other people and glory to Thy name.* AMEN.

Note. In recent times some have doubted whether Paul was the writer of this letter: (1) Because in form, in words and expressions used, and in style of writing, it is quite different from other letters that we know to be Paul's. (2) Because it is very similar to Colossians, and because of the way it is connected with other New Testament writings (especially those of Paul). (3) Because there are things in Ephesians that are thought more likely to have been written at a later date than the apostle's life-time, and other things that are thought unlikely to have been written by him.

One suggestion is that twenty or thirty years after Paul's death, a person who knew and loved Paul's letters (especially Colossians) wrote this work in his name to form an introduction to the collection of letters that he had made. Such views, and the arguments for and against them, may be found in more detailed commentaries on Ephesians.

We have assumed that Paul did indeed write this letter, and believe this for the following reasons: (1) Because in quite early days the church accepted it without question as Paul's. (2) Because there seems to be no compelling argument why Paul could not have written everything that the letter contains. (3) Because its similarities to the other letters that bear Paul's name are best explained by regarding Paul as writer; and in particular, the close connection with Colossians is most naturally explained if we think of Ephesians as written at the same time, but not needing to deal with the particular problems that the church at Colossae faced. (4) Because the letter is too great to be the work of a person writing in the name of Paul, and trying to copy his work. We would say, however, that the study of the contents and inspired teaching of the letter is far more important than the question of who wrote it.

Further Study. Compare with this first verse the way that Paul speaks of himself in the beginning of his other letters, and in 1 Corinthians 15:9–10, Galatians 1:13–16, and 1 Timothy 1:12–16, and the way that other apostles and New Testament writers speak of themselves (*e.g.* in John 13:23; 20:2; 21:24; James 1:1; 1 Peter 1:1; 5:1; 2 Peter 1:1; Revelation 1:1, 9).

Study 2. THE READERS

To the saints who are also faithful in Christ Jesus' (1:1b).

It seems likely that this letter was sent to Ephesus, but at the same time sent to other churches as well

(see Note below). We should imagine Tychicus the
messenger (6:21) going from place to place, and reading
the letter in Ephesus, in Laodicea, in Colossae, in
Hierapolis, and in other churches of the same district.
Where these readers were, however, is less important
to us than the three things that the apostle now says
about them.

a. They are saints

We usually use this word only for the greatest
Christians who have ever lived. Paul, however, did not
write this letter just to a select few, but to all in the
churches. For according to the New Testament, all
are 'called to be saints' (Romans 1:7). The Greek
word in the New Testament is the same as 'holy', and
means 'set apart' or 'dedicated'. The same is true in
the Old Testament, where places or things are 'holy'
when they are set apart for the worship of God. The
Christian, in the same way, is set apart for the service
of God in his daily life and work. The moral and
spiritual standards of life – what we call 'holiness' –
follow from that. The holiness of God means that He is
apart from all evil; and He says to all who would be
His people, 'You shall be holy' (you shall be 'saints'),
'for I am holy' (see Leviticus 11:44 and 1 Peter 1:16).
Dedication to God, and to His standards of truth,
purity and love, is every Christian's calling.

b. They are faithful

Faith is the first step of the Christian life. By faith a
person accepts God's salvation (2:8). Faith is the
necessary attitude of the whole life of the Christian
(3:17). 'Without faith it is impossible to please' God
(Hebrews 11:6). But Paul thinks of his readers, not only

as having faith, but as those who are called to faithfulness. When faith endures through all difficulties, disappointment and ridicule of men, then that is faithfulness.

c. They are in Christ Jesus

This little phrase is so important that Paul uses it (or something very near it) thirty-seven times in this letter. He does not mean just that his readers have faith in Christ Jesus. Their life is *in Him*. The Christian life, as Jesus Himself said to His disciples, is a matter of 'I in you' and 'you in Me' (see John 15:4–7). As the fish lives in the sea, the bird in the air, the unborn child in its mother's womb, so the very place of our life is Christ. From Him we have life itself, strength, and all things. If we are true to Him, we will not move beyond the place of His will and purpose for us, or away from His love and guidance and inspiration. However difficult it may be in the place where we live, we can remember always that spiritually our lives are in Christ. With our hearts at rest in Him and strong in Him, we can face any difficulty or danger.

Prayer. *Lord, Thou hast called us not only to know Thee and to believe in Thee, but to abide in Thee, and in Thee to find life, wisdom, strength, and all that we need. May no thoughts of pride, nor love of this world, draw us away from Thee, but in our daily lives make us faithful; and by Thy presence with us and in us make us more like Thee in holiness, for the glory of Thy name.* AMEN.

Note. There are four things that make us think that this letter was not sent originally just to Ephesus: (1) Some of the very oldest copies of the letter that we have omit the words 'at Ephesus' in 1:1. (2) The whole letter,

as we have seen, is more general than we would expect
if it were written to any one church with its particular
problems. (3) If Paul was writing to a church in a place
where he spent as long as he did in Ephesus (see Acts
19 and 20), we would expect many personal messages,
and in fact we find none. (4) Some things Paul could
hardly have written to people whom he knew as well as
he knew the members of the church at Ephesus (see
especially 1:15; 3:2; 4:20–21). Rather it seems likely
that this letter is the one referred to in Colossians 4:16
as coming 'from Laodicea', and that Paul wrote it
when he wrote Colossians, and gave it to Tychicus to
take round to the various churches of the Roman
provinces of Asia, the area that included Ephesus,
Laodicea and Colossae.

Further Study. Underline or make a list of the places
in this letter where the phrase 'in Christ' is used.

Study 3. A GREETING THAT IS A PRAYER

'Grace to you and peace from God our Father and the Lord Jesus Christ' (1:2).

The usual greeting of the Greeks whose language
Paul used as he wrote this letter was a word connected
with 'grace'. We find it in Acts 15:23; 23:26 and James
1:1. The common greeting of Paul's own people, the
Jews, and of many other peoples, was 'peace' (see Luke
10:5). Paul did not just let these common greetings
slip off his tongue without meaning. He put them in a
special way, and made them a prayer for the grace and
peace that come to men 'from God our Father and the
Lord Jesus Christ'. In fact 'grace', used twelve times in
Ephesians, and 'peace', used seven times, we may call
twin subjects of this letter.

15

a. Grace

In three particular ways Paul thinks of grace as he writes in this letter of God's free gifts, and of Christ's work for us. (1) First, and most important, it is the undeserved favour of God that He shows in receiving us sinners, and in making us His sons. In 2:4–9 the apostle expresses this most fully. (2) Then, those who by grace are accepted with God receive by His Spirit the gifts of grace – abilities, opportunities, powers, to do His work. 'Grace was given', Paul says in 4:7, 'to each of us according to the measure of Christ's gift.' In His wisdom He gives to some one gift, to some another, but all 'for the equipment of the saints, for the work of ministry, for building up the body of Christ' (4:12; see also Romans 12:3, 6; 15:15; Galatians 1:15). (3) Then there was another special way in which Paul thought of the grace of God. It was the privilege of being called to work for Him, and to tell out His gospel. This is his subject in the first part of chapter 3. It was because of God's grace, His undeserved love and favour, that the knowledge of the Saviour could come not only to Israel, but to all people. It was because of God's grace, grace more wonderful than Paul could describe, that he (and we like him) should be called to preach Christ to men. What a privilege to be His messenger!

b. Peace

The word 'peace' also includes very much of what Paul wants to write. (1) In the first place the peace which is the very subject of the gospel is peace with God. Jesus Christ came to be 'our peace' (2:14), to make peace 'by the blood of his cross' (Colossians 1:20). By our sins we had made ourselves enemies of God, rejecting His ways and despising His word. There was no peace in our hearts. We needed reconciliation, but could not make it ourselves. Only God could do it, as we shall see later, and He did it in His Son Jesus Christ. (2) When we have that peace with God, we find also peace in our hearts; but in this letter Paul says less of this heart-peace than in such passages as Philippians 4:7. He says more here of peace between one person and another in the fellowship of the Christian family. This is a great gift of God, to be received, and then to be kept. There is one way to God, one body into which we come – there must be no more division. We who have received peace with God, and who are called to witness to it, must no longer quarrel among ourselves.

Such grace and peace Paul writes of, and prays as he writes and as he greets his Christian friends. We too are called to be grace-bringers, peace-makers, as we go out into each day, as we greet our friends, write our letters, and do the common things of the home, of daily work, and of social life.

Prayer. *Lord, deep in our hearts may we know Thy grace and peace, and in loving thanksgiving may we be witnesses to what Thou hast done for us, and messengers of Thy grace and peace to others, through Jesus Christ our Saviour.* AMEN.

Further Study. 1. Compare with this the introductory greetings in other New Testament letters.

2. Study the use of the words 'grace' and 'peace' in the rest of this letter.

1:3-14. PRAISE FOR GOD'S PURPOSE AND BLESSINGS IN CHRIST

THESE VERSES are like a great hymn of praise telling of the wonderful blessings of God that come to men in Christ. The apostle goes on from one to another – God has chosen us, He has made us His sons, He has redeemed and forgiven us, He has brought us to know His purpose, He has given us the Holy Spirit now, and the promise of His perfect inheritance in the end.

Study 4. THE BEGINNING AND THE END OF GOD'S BLESSINGS

'Blessed be the God and Father of our Lord Jesus Christ, who has blessed us in Christ with every spiritual blessing in the heavenly places, even as he chose us in him before the foundation of the world, that we should be holy and blameless before him' (1:3-4).

At the beginning of these verses that speak of the great blessings that are in Christ, the Almighty is spoken of as 'the God . . . of our Lord Jesus Christ', because in Christ He is made known to us (John 1:18). Christ is also the Son through whom we come to the Father. Every material blessing we owe to God, as Creator and Provider, but our thoughts are turned here to His spiritual gifts, and in these two verses we should note three things about them.

a. Blessings are given in the heavenly places

Five times in the Epistle we find this phrase (here and 1:20; 2:6; 3:10; 6:12). Life 'in Christ' means a heavenly life even while we are on earth. The blessings for which Paul praises God are not future – God 'has blessed us' with these things. If we are 'in Christ' (see on verse 1), we have eternal life, the life of heaven, while we are on earth. We are lifted up so that our lives are no longer limited by the things on earth (see 2:6 and Colossians 3:1–3). Our citizenship is in heaven (Philippians 3:20), while we remain on earth. We are to live in this world in the power of heaven (6:10), by the standards of heaven (Romans 12:2), and with the blessings of a heavenly inheritance.

b. Blessings begin with God's choice of us to be His own

Long before we were born, indeed 'before the foundation of the world', God chose us. What can that mean? We may not be able to understand it fully, but at least it means that God has an eternal purpose for us, a purpose not limited by the changing things of our lives in this world. It means also that all we have and are depends on Him. The Epistle to the Hebrews (6:19) speaks of our hope in God as an 'anchor of the soul'; it holds us to the unchanging things of eternity as the anchor of a great ship holds it in the angry seas. In the storms of life we can remain firm. Often we are tempted to be depressed or discouraged; we feel so much depends on us, and we are weak and fall. It does not all depend on us, because we can depend on our Lord. The thought of this also keeps us from pride. Our faith is very important, but it rests on what He has planned and done, and not on anything in ourselves.

c. The end and purpose of every blessing

To some people the matter of God's choice – or predestination – brings great difficulties. Why, they ask, has God chosen some and not others? Paul does not ask this kind of question. Always he preached, 'Whoever wishes to do so may come and receive God's blessings.' Then he showed that God's choice of us means that our Christian lives depend on the Rock of ages, on God Himself, and not just on the family into which we were born, or the friends who could help us. He has chosen us, moreover, not only that we might be happy, enjoying the blessings of His salvation, but that we might live to His praise – 'that we should be holy and blameless before him'. He uses first the word that we have studied already in verse 1 – we are to be saints, 'holy', dedicated men and women. We are to be 'blameless'. The meaning of this word is 'without blemish'. In Old Testament days the animals sacrificed by the Jews had to be physically 'without blemish' (Leviticus 1:3,10, *etc.*). Jesus Himself in His life and character was 'without blemish' (Hebrews 9:14 and 1 Peter 1:19). We are to be like Him, and Romans 8:29 says what this verse says when it speaks of us as 'predestined to be conformed to the image' of Christ.

Prayer. *Lord of all power, the Beginning and the End of all things, we praise Thee for Thy eternal purpose. Help us to live on earth the heavenly life that Thou hast planned for us, in full dedication to Thee, and in true love for all men. May sin not mark or spoil our lives, nor the standards of this world control us, for Thy holy name's sake.* AMEN.

Further Study. What reasons do the following passages give for God's choice of those who are His people? Deuteronomy 7:6–8; Isaiah 42:1, 6–7; 43:21;

John 15:16; Romans 8:29; 2 Thessalonians 2:13; 1 Peter 2:9.

Study 5. SONS OF GOD

God has 'destined us in love to be his sons through Jesus Christ, according to the purpose of his will, to the praise of his glorious grace which he freely bestowed on us in the Beloved. In him we have redemption through his blood, the forgiveness of our trespasses, according to the riches of his grace' (1:5-7).

The first words of verse 5 show that the apostle's subject is still the eternal purpose of God. Almighty God has an amazing plan for us. He has appointed us to a destiny. He has offered to us the greatest privilege that anyone can imagine.

a. The privilege: that we should be sons of God

Genesis 1 tells us that this was God's purpose from the beginning. Man was different from every other creature because he was made in the likeness of God. He is a creature indeed, but with a likeness to God and a nearness to God that no other has. Like a son with his father, he is able to speak to God and hear His word. Yet man, with the God-given freedom that went with this, chose not to keep this great privilege of fellowship with the Almighty. He preferred his own way, and did not wish to hear the Father's voice, nor realize His presence. The parable of the runaway son (Luke 15:11-24) tells the story of us all. We think that our ways of enjoying ourselves are better than living with the Father and doing His will. Yet our Almighty Father, like the father in that wonderful parable,

wishes to receive us back as sons. We have lost all right
to that position, but the process of adoption shows what
God wishes to do. An adopted child has no right, by
birth or by his action, to a place in the home, as he
really belongs to another; but he is admitted freely and
fully to the place and privilege of a son. (See John 1:12;
Romans 8:15; Galatians 4:5.)

b. The means of this privilege

'Grace' we found in the very beginning of this
Epistle, and Paul repeats it here, 'his glorious grace',
'the riches of his grace', 'grace which he freely bestowed
on us in the Beloved'. The Father has one beloved Son,
One faithful to Him in all things. This One came into a
sinful world of runaway sons, to win them back, to
redeem them. For our rebellion takes away from us the
right to be sons. Only by the Father's forgiveness can
we be received back. But how could a righteous God
forgive, without treating lightly the sin of our rebellion?
Only in the costly way of bearing Himself that sin of
rebellion. 'Through his blood' is a phrase that makes us
think of the whole system of sacrifice. Deep in his heart
(by the work of God there), man in almost every race
has felt the need to offer some sacrifice, to regain
fellowship with the god he worships. The Old Testament shows this in a way that is free from the false ideas
of the heathen about God. The Jews learnt there to
sacrifice an animal 'without blemish' because their own
lives were so full of the blemishes of sin. But ultimately
the blood of animals could not take away sin. The Old
Testament sacrifices pointed forward to the only
sacrifice that can take away sin – the sacrifice of the
sinless Son of God. 'Redeem' is another word that we
can understand best by thinking back to the Old Testament. We read there of the redeeming of property,

the redeeming of the slave, and we read of the redemption of Israel from slavery, first in Egypt and then in Babylon. So we were slaves of sin, unable to free ourselves, but now in and through that same beloved Son, we have redemption and freedom. Grace, grace, grace – no wonder Paul repeats the word in joyful praise.

c. The purpose of the privilege

Again Paul will not let us rest in a privilege. A son has more responsibilities in the house than a servant. He is made like his father – he must *be* like his father (see Matthew 5:44–45; Luke 6:35). He has to uphold the honour of his father. It is 'according to the purpose of his will', that is, by God's favour and love we become sons of God. It is also that we should be 'to the praise of his glorious grace'. These words come as a chorus here, and then again in verses 12 and 14. In Old Testament days God said about Israel, they are 'the people whom I formed for myself that they might declare my praise' (Isaiah 43:21). That is the purpose that He has for us – to live to His praise, to show forth to others His glory, His grace.

Prayer. *Lord Jesus, at a cost greater than we can ever understand Thou hast made us who are sinners to be sons of God. May we, in love that increases from day to day, praise Thee by the thoughts of our hearts, by our words and by our actions, for Thy great name's sake.* AMEN.

Notes. 1. God's 'glory' is the showing forth of Himself as He is; above all, therefore, it is the showing forth of His goodness and grace. See Exodus 33:18–19; 34:5–7.
    2. The 'Beloved' is a title, but Colossians 1:13 shows

23

us that it means the Son who is deeply loved by His Father. So here it shows the cost to the Father of our salvation. Compare John 3:16.

3. Often in the New Testament use of the word 'redemption' the main thought is of our being set free from the slavery of sin; but sometimes the cost of our freedom is emphasized. See 1 Corinthians 6:20; 7:23; 1 Peter 1:18–19.

Further Study. From the following passages study the Old Testament background of redemption: Leviticus 25:25–27, 47–49; Numbers 18:15–16; Exodus 15:13; Deuteronomy 7:8; Isaiah 48:20; 52:9.

Study 6. KNOWLEDGE OF GOD'S PURPOSE

'He lavished (this grace) upon us. For he has made known to us in all wisdom and insight the mystery of his will, according to his purpose which he set forth in Christ as a plan for the fullness of time, to unite all things in him, things in heaven and things on earth' (1:8–10).

We have seen that 'grace' is the key word of verses 6 and 7. By grace, freely given to us in the beloved Son, we are forgiven and made sons by adoption. But Paul has more to say of the results of grace.

a. God's wisdom is known

Verses 8 and 9 go on to speak of God's grace poured on us giving 'wisdom and insight'. God in His grace forgives us the past, but He also gives us light for all the path of life. Jesus said, 'I am the light of the world'; and

He added, 'he who follows me will not walk in darkness, but will have the light of life' (John 8:12). He helps us to know the truth, all the truth that we need for our daily lives. 'Wisdom and insight', Paul says here. 'Wisdom' is the truth about the deepest things of life – what God is like, and what is His purpose for us. 'Insight' is practical knowledge that leads us to act rightly in the common things of every day; it is God's gift for us to know how to act even in the little things. Both wisdom and insight He gives – 'the ability to see the great ultimate truths of eternity and to solve the problems of each moment of time' (Barclay).

b. God's truth is revealed

Then, as Paul speaks of this wisdom and insight that come from God, he uses a word that comes again five times in this letter, the word 'mystery'. We usually think of a mystery as something strange and hidden. In the New Testament it is nearly always something that is revealed or made plain. It is what we certainly could not know by ourselves (see 1 Corinthians 2:6–16), but God shows it to all who desire to understand. Grace is the right word again, because it is in His love and pity that He has not left us in darkness, but has shown us His way and His will.

c. God's purpose is shown

We have seen that the purpose of God is the great subject of this letter. Verse 10 now gives a summary of God's 'plan'. The word that is translated as 'plan' is connected with the word for 'house'. It pictures the head of the house making arrangements for the running of the household. God has an arrangement for His house, which is the world, or rather, the whole universe. His arrangement, His purpose will come to pass in the 'fullness of time'. That means that the times are in His hands, and He will carry out His perfect plan at the perfect time. It sometimes seems that men who do not care for God at all are in control in the world; but in 'the fullness of time' it will be clear that God has been at work all along. Then His great work will be seen to be the uniting or summing up of all things in Christ. You may sum up a column of figures and give the total. You may sum up a speech. Romans 13:8–10 speaks of the summing up of the whole law in the one word 'love'. When there is a summing up, all the different parts, scattered and divided before, are brought together and become one. The world in which we live – the whole universe in fact – is one. It came from the hand of the one God, and in His work there is order and beauty. But because of sin there is now disorder. We see among men deep and terrible divisions – divisions between men of different colour, race, tribe or class. God's purpose is to bring back all things to His plan, and so to unity; each thing, each part of the whole is to be put to its proper use. This work He is doing in Christ, who came (as the next chapter of the letter shows more clearly) to bring sinful men back to Himself, and also into unity and fellowship among themselves. So these verses remind us that the almighty God, the Lord and Creator of all, has a purpose for men. He wants us to know His ways. He wants to guide us each day of our lives, that we may live according to His perfect plan. And still more wonderful, He wants us to have a part in the working out of His great purpose of bringing all things back to find their life and unity in Him, by Jesus Christ (see 2 Corinthians 10:5).

Prayer. *O God, Thou has called us to know and to share Thy great purpose. Help us, so that the details of our daily lives*

may be ordered by Thee, and that we may do Thy work, Thy
will, Thy good pleasure, in Jesus Christ our Lord. AMEN.

Note. Verse 10 should not be taken to mean that all
will be saved in the end, and that the world is getting
nearer and nearer to this fulfilment. We must take this
verse along with the other teaching of Paul and of the
whole New Testament. We see that men's destiny
depends on their acceptance or rejection of God's
salvation; and the world is shown to be the place of
increasing conflict between the people of God and the
forces of evil. Before the end there will be bitter conflict.
Then there will be judgment, and the perfect fulfilment
of what God has sought to do among men all the time.

Further Study. Study carefully the following references to the 'mystery' of God: Romans 16:25-26; Ephesians 3:3-4; Colossians 1:26-27; 2:2.

Study 7.
THE PRIVILEGES OF GOD'S PEOPLE

'In him, according to the purpose of him who
accomplishes all things according to the counsel
of his will, we who first hoped in Christ have been
destined and appointed to live for the praise of
his glory. In him you also, who have heard the
word of truth, the gospel of your salvation, and
have believed in him, were sealed with the pro-
mised Holy Spirit, which is the guarantee of our
inheritance until we acquire possession of it, to
the praise of his glory' (1:11-14).
These verses take up some of the key words of the
earlier verses – 'destined', 'purpose', 'his will', 'the
praise of his glory'. We see more of the spiritual

blessings God has given us, and others prepared for us; but we are also reminded of our responsibilities.

a. God's people

When Paul says again that we were 'destined and appointed', he is saying that by God's choice, and in His great purpose, we are made His people. In the first place Paul is taking up what was said in the Old Testament of the Jews; they were God's people (see Deuteronomy 4:20; 9:29; 32:9). When he says 'we who first hoped in Christ', he is speaking of those same people, Paul's people, who had hoped for the Christ before His coming. But now he says that Gentiles (non-Jews) have come to share these privileges (compare 1 Peter 2:9) – 'you also' he says in verse 13. *Now* all of us who have faith in Christ, whatever our race, class, sex, age, colour, are God's people. (Chapter 2 will have more to say about this.) This is our high privilege, but with it there is a great responsibility, to live as those who belong to Him, 'to the praise of his glory'.

b. Our inheritance

God in His amazing love and goodness makes us His people. Paul goes on to say that this means that He offers to us a great inheritance. This letter in fact often speaks of the 'riches' that are ours in Christ (see verses 7 and 18; 2:7 and 3:16), heavenly riches which are infinitely more valuable than all the riches of the world. (See Matthew 6:19–20 and 1 Timothy 6:17–19.) They are heavenly riches, but we have a great part of them now. For we 'have heard the word of truth', which is 'the gospel' of our 'salvation'. We know that as we trust in Christ, we are made free from the penalty and power of sin. And this real freedom we must take to others.

c. The promise

We have part of the inheritance now, but part is still future. Ultimately we shall be freed from the very presence of sin and from all the stains and sorrows and troubles that sin has caused. We have the promise now of the full inheritance, of this final salvation, and not only the word of promise, but also some foretaste of what we shall enjoy. We cannot yet see God face to face, but we can know His presence. God the Holy Spirit is given to live in our lives. He guides us, He gives us strength, joy, love, and every blessing. (See Acts 1:8; Galatians 5:22.) He is also called the 'seal'. For just as the seal is used to mark a thing as belonging to a particular person, and to show that it is carried undamaged, so the Holy Spirit marks us, and makes us sure that we belong to God Himself. (See Galatians 4:6–7 and Romans 8:15–16.) He makes us sure that we will be kept by His power to the coming day of the Lord. He is also the 'guarantee'. This word 'guarantee' was used in New Testament days for the part payment for something bought, or of a debt – the promise that the rest would be paid. In this way the Holy Spirit is God's promise.

Prayer. *O Lord our God, in Thy great love Thou hast made us Thy people, and hast given us heavenly riches. Help us to believe, to hope, and to live to witness to the gospel of our salvation, until that day when we see Thee face to face, and praise Thy glory for ever and ever.* AMEN.

Further Study. Study the other passages in the New Testament which speak of the Holy Spirit as 'seal' or 'guarantee' – Ephesians 4:30; 2 Corinthians 1:22; 5:5 – and see the similar teaching of Romans 8:16–17, 23.

1:15–23. THE WEALTH OF THE CHRISTIAN'S INHERITANCE

Most of the letters which were written in the time of the apostles began with a greeting, and then had thanksgiving and prayer. A letter might open in words like these: 'John . . . to his dear sister, greeting. When I heard from you, I gave thanks to God that you were well, and continue to have you in my prayers.' Paul followed the usual custom, but with him the prayer and thanksgiving, as well as the greeting, had deep meaning. They were Christian prayer and praise.

Study 8. PRAISE AND PRAYER

'For this reason, because I have heard of your faith in the Lord Jesus and your love toward all the saints, I do not cease to give thanks for you, remembering you in my prayers, that the God of our Lord Jesus Christ, the Father of glory, may give you a spirit of wisdom and of revelation in the knowledge of him' (1:15–17).

Paul constantly taught the Christians to whom he wrote his letters to thank God as well as to bring their petitions to Him, to join praise and prayer (see Philippians 4:6; 1 Thessalonians 5:18). He set a good example in this.

a. Praise

Paul not only praised God for all that he had come

30

to know of His love and grace and power and greatness. He also tried to find things in the church to which he wrote for which he could give thanks to God. There might have been many weaknesses, and many reasons for criticism. Criticism usually comes to our lips more easily than praise. Paul first looked to see God's work in others, for which he could offer praise. In this case he could sincerely thank God for the faith that bound them to the Lord, and for the fact that because of this faith these Christians were no longer living self-centred lives, but were showing thoughtfulness and love to others. When we look for things in others that we can commend, and for which we can thank God, then our hearts will be kept pure from unkind criticism, and we will be a strength to our fellows by our words of encouragement.

b. Prayer

Paul gives us an example also in the constancy of his prayers. He tells us to 'pray constantly' (see 6:18 and 1 Thessalonians 5:17); and he could say to these Christians, 'I do not cease to give thanks for you, remembering you in my prayers.' He could say without pride or insincerity that among all the burdens, trials, persecutions, and dangers that the work of an apostle brought to him, the most constant of all his cares was that for all the churches (2 Corinthians 11:28). That meant above all a life of prayer and constant inter-cession for them. Surely that is the reason why Paul accomplished so much. If there is little prayer, there will be little lasting work for God's kingdom; if there is much prayer, then much work of eternal value will be done.

Paul knew that, whether he was among these Christians, or far away from them, he could still pray for them. He could do this work still in his old age and in his prison, chained to a Roman soldier.

c. The God to whom we pray

When the psalmists wanted to strengthen the faith of their people in time of need and trouble, they did so by speaking of God's greatness, and of what He had done in the past. (For example see Psalms 78; 135; 136; 146.) Before Paul prayed, he praised God for what He had done already. Often also he added a descriptive phrase to the name of God, so that those who read his prayers might be helped to think more of the greatness of Him to whom they prayed (compare 3:14-15). Here he speaks of Him as 'the God of our Lord Jesus Christ'. He is the God whom we know in Christ. When we see the power of Christ, the love of Christ, we see the almighty power and the unfailing love of the God to whom we pray. When we hear the word of Christ, 'Ask, and it will be given you' (Matthew 7:7), we know it is the word of God. God is also 'the Father of glory', and source of all power and greatness and majesty that we know in creation, in His care over all things, and in His redeeming work of which so much has been said in verses 1-14.

Prayer. *Lord, help us to see Thy glory, and to praise Thee for Thy work in the hearts of men. So set us free from bitterness and pride; and in every time of temptation, and for every need of our fellows, make us constant in prayer and in loving service, through Jesus Christ our Saviour.* AMEN.

Further Study. Study the following passages for Paul's teaching about prayer and thanksgiving: Ephesians 5:19-20; Romans 12:12; Philippians 4:6-7; Colossians 4:2; 1 Thessalonians 5:17-18.

Study 9. THE PRAYER FOR WISDOM

I pray that God 'may give you a spirit of wisdom and of revelation in the knowledge of him, having the eyes of your hearts enlightened, that you may know what is the hope to which he has called you, what are the riches of his glorious inheritance in the saints, and what is the immeasurable greatness of his power . . .' (I:I7–I9).

We can learn much from the prayers of the apostle Paul, and from those parts of his letters where he tells us what he prayed for the churches to which he wrote. When we think of our own prayers beside his, we realize that often we pray for small things, when there are far greater things for which we should ask. Notice three things here.

a. The light of truth

At the beginning of Solomon's reign, we read that God told the young king that he could ask from Him whatever he wished. As he thought of the great work before him, and his own weakness, he prayed for 'an understanding mind'. God was pleased with that prayer, and fully answered it (see I Kings 3). Paul made the same prayer for wisdom and understanding; and we have seen that to him 'wisdom' meant the understanding of the meaning and purpose of life (see on verse 9). The words that he adds also have important things to teach us. The word 'revelation' reminds us that such wisdom cannot come just by our searching and study, but only as God in His grace shows His glorious truth to us. That wisdom, moreover, is not just knowledge of facts and ideas. It is the knowledge of God Himself. That means knowing Him as a Person. It means fellowship with Him; and it means eternal life (John 17:3). Such wisdom is indeed light for our eyes, light in the world's darkness; and if we follow that light, we shall never stumble.

b. The hope of His calling

Paul prayed that these Christians to whom he wrote might have wisdom to know the hope of God's calling. There were two things that helped and kept Paul in times of great trial and difficulty. One was the hope that he had in Christ. For he could say, 'I consider that the sufferings of this present time are not worth comparing with the glory that is to be revealed to us' (Romans 8:18). The second thing was that he was sure that God had called him. We saw this in verse 1 when we studied the way that Paul spoke of himself as 'an apostle of Christ Jesus by the will of God'. Often we speak of *our* calling. Notice that Paul says here it is *God's* calling. He was called personally to be the representative of the King of kings. If the eternal God has called us, made us His children and His messengers, given us His Spirit now and the hope of life with Him for ever, then there is nothing that the world can do to us that we need fear.

c. The riches of His inheritance

Then Paul prays that they may be wise to know 'the riches of his glorious inheritance in the saints'. 'In the saints' means among the saints, among those who by faith are God's people. (See Acts 20:32.) In studying verses 11-14, we considered the meaning of the inheritance of God's people. If we know that so rich an inheritance is in our hands, then poverty, persecution, disappointment or even disaster in this life will not shake our faith. The riches of living as God's sons and daughters are infinitely greater than all the riches of the world. And those riches of God are for us. It is a prayer worth praying, when the pull of temptation is strong, or when the world seems against us, that we (and our fellow-Christians) may know the riches and glory of what He offers us now, and what He has prepared for us.

Prayer. *Lord, help us to know Thee, Thy glory, Thy grace, Thy great gifts. So with faith, hope, and confidence in Thee, may we let no discouragement or difficulty turn us aside from the path of obedience until that path reaches the joy of Thy presence for ever and ever.* AMEN.

Further Study. Study the things for which Paul prays in the following passages: Ephesians 3:14-19; Philippians 1:9-11; Colossians 1:9-12; 1 Thessalonians 3:12-13; 2 Thessalonians 1:11-12.

Study 10. THE PRAYER FOR POWER

I pray that you may know 'what is the immeasurable greatness of his power in us who believe, according to the working of his great might which he accomplished in Christ when he raised him from the dead and made him sit at his right hand in the heavenly places, far above all rule and authority and power and dominion, and above every name that is named, not only in this age but also in that which is to come' (1:19-21).

From verse 15 Paul has been telling his readers how he prays for them. He asks that they may have wisdom – wisdom to know the hope of God's calling, the riches of the glory of His inheritance, and now, thirdly, wisdom to realize His power.

35

a. The power of God

One word is not sufficient for Paul to describe God's power. He uses several words. He speaks first of 'the immeasurable greatness of his power', the never-failing supplies of His power that we can have. Then he speaks of 'his great might' that makes us able to do difficult things and to face trying situations. But this power is not like that of an engine pulling or pushing a great load. It is power in us; it is inner strength (see 3:16). The word Paul uses is the word from which we have our English word 'energy'. It means 'in-working' (it is used also in 3:7; 4:16; Philippians 3:21 and Colossians 1:29). Paul is saying that, if we believe, if we let Him live and rule in our lives, He will work in us, energize us, and give us inner supplies of power.

b. The power of God shown in Christ

Even these various words that Paul has used are not sufficient to describe God's power that can be ours. He calls us to look at the one Life in which that power has been at work perfectly and without hindrance. Men were allowed to take that One, and nail Him to a cross. He gave His life, but He could not remain in the grave. The Father raised Him from the dead. That is the greatest way that we can see the power of God – the power that is offered to us. It means power over every work of evil, over every evil force, over death itself. Paul prayed for himself, 'that I may know him, and the power of his resurrection' (Philippians 3:10). He made the same prayer for others; and we can make it our prayer.

c. Power over all things

God the Father not only raised Christ from the dead,

but also exalted Him to His right hand, and set Him 'far above all rule and authority and power and dominion, and above every name that is named, not only in this age but also in that which is to come'. This is so important, because by it we know that all things are under His control. For the person who lives 'in Christ' and has His power, there is nothing to fear – no power of man, no spiritual power of evil, no trouble or danger that the future may bring. Remember the way that Paul put this in Romans 8:38-39, 'I am sure that neither death, nor life, nor angels, nor principalities, nor things present, nor things to come, nor powers, nor height, nor depth, nor anything else in all creation, will be able to separate us from the love of God in Christ Jesus our Lord.'

Prayer. *Lord God Almighty, the Source of all power, may we in our weakness receive in us the promised power of Thy Spirit, the power of Christ and His resurrection. So may we never be ashamed of Thy name, may we never fail through fear, nor turn aside from the life of love and service to which Thou hast called us in Jesus our Lord.* AMEN.

Notes. 1. Most frequently the New Testament does not simply say 'Christ rose from the dead', but 'God raised him'. See Acts 2:24, 32; 3:15; 4:10. This shows the Father's approval of all His life. It shows Him as the Son of God and Lord of all, and it also shows the power of God.

2. The New Testament also often speaks, as it does here, of Christ being exalted and set 'at the right hand' of the Father. By this we are not to think of a particular 'place' where He is (and so in no other place), but the words express His authority and rule as Lord of all.

Further Study. In the following passages study what

is said about the power of God, and what its effects should be in the lives of men: Acts 1:8; Colossians 1:11, 29; 1 Peter 1:5; 2 Peter 1:3.

Study 11. CHRIST AND HIS CHURCH

'And he has put all things under his feet and has made him the head over all things for the church, which is his body, the fullness of him who fills all in all' (1:22–23).

These verses are still Paul's prayer but, for the encouragement of his readers, he emphasizes that Christ is Lord of all, and tells what it means to belong to His church. In the New Testament the church is never thought of simply as the collection of people who believe in Christ. It is a community of people with a special place in God's purpose. They are the 'household of God', 'the people of God', 'the temple of God'. And here they are described in a way that surpasses all these other descriptions.

a. The church is the body of Christ

Christians are like members of a body, having the same life flowing through them. Since the church is the body of Christ, that life is the life of Christ. If they have not that life, they are not truly members of His body (see Romans 8:9; John 15:6), even though outwardly they may be members of a Christian organization. The church, moreover, is Christ's instrument in the world, doing His work, representing Him. In Acts 1:1 Luke refers back to his Gospel as the story of the things 'that Jesus *began* to do and teach'; he meant that the story of the church is the *continuing* of what Jesus does and teaches in the world. Of course there were things that the Lord did 'in the body of his flesh' which cannot be repeated, supremely what He did by His death and resurrection for our salvation. But in other ways the calling of Christians is to do Christ's work in the world as members of His body.

b. The church is the fullness of Christ

The words that close the chapter are difficult words, and they have been explained in different ways. What does it mean that the church is the fullness of Christ? Christ is called 'the fullness of God' because He is and expresses fully what God is (Colossians 1:19; 2:9). The church cannot be the fullness of Christ in just that way. But we must have no lesser aim than to know and to receive Him fully (see 3:19; 4:13 and John 1:16), and to express Him fully in the world. How can the world see and know Him today except through us?

'He has no hands but our hands, to do His work today,
   He has no feet but our feet to lead men in His way.'

He seeks to fill all things. We must let Him do what He is always seeking to do – to fill us with Himself, His Spirit (5:18), and so to show Himself, His will and His word through us in the world.

c. The church has Christ for its Head

We can, however, only be His body, and grow and increase spiritually, as we make Him our Head, whose orders we obey. (Compare 4:15; 5:23 and Colossians 1:18; 2:19.) But this passage gives us a further thought. Christ is Head of the church, but He is also 'head over all things for the church'. All things are under His control. So, if we are His people, we have His victory on

His authority. Before the Lord sent out His disciples, He assured them of this. 'All authority in heaven and on earth has been given to me. Go therefore. . . .' (Matthew 28:18–19.) He says to us, as He sends us out day by day to work and witness for Him, 'Go with My power and My authority. Be sure that if you abide in Me, and do My will, nothing on earth can overcome you, and nothing need fill you with fear. Difficulties and trials, sorrows and sickness, need never defeat you. I will give you victory in them all. I am with you always.'

Prayer. *O fill me with Thy fullness, Lord,*
Until my very heart o'erflow
In kindling thought and glowing word,
Thy love to tell, Thy praise to show.
                                        AMEN.

Notes. 1. Verse 22 uses the words of Psalm 8:6. In the Psalm they applied to man, but the words are perfectly true now only of the one Man Jesus Christ. They can become true for us through Him. See Hebrews 2:5–10.

2. In verse 23 some have understood 'the fullness of Christ' to mean that which fills Christ. 'Until He is united to us, the Son of God reckons Himself in some sense imperfect' (Calvin). So Paul speaks of the sufferings of Christ being filled up by the sufferings of the church in Colossians 1:24. It seems, however, more the emphasis of the New Testament that Christ seeks to fill the church than to be filled by it. See especially 4:10,13,16.

Further Study. Study the different things that are meant when the following passages speak of the church as the body of Christ: 2:16; 3:6; 4:4, 12, 16; Romans 12:4–8; 1 Corinthians 12; Colossians 1:18.

2:1–10. THE RICHES OF GOD'S GRACE

Chapter 1 has ended with Paul's prayer that his readers may know the power of Christ's resurrection, and that they may share His victory and live under His authority. Now the apostle goes on to show man's deep and utter need of the new life that only Christ crucified and risen can give; because, as he is, man without Christ is dead in sin.

Study 12. DEATH THROUGH SIN

'And you he made alive, when you were dead through the trespasses and sins in which you once walked, following the course of this world, following the prince of the power of the air, the spirit that is now at work in the sons of disobedience. Among these we all once lived in the passions of our flesh, following the desires of body and mind, and so we were by nature children of wrath, like the rest of mankind' (2:1–3).

As Paul wrote it, the words 'you he made alive' did not come till verse 5. Verses 1–3 told only what we were like, in our sin, apart from Christ.

a. Lifeless because of sin

Genesis 1:26–27 tells us that God made man in His

likeness. God breathed into him the breath of life, and
he became a living being (Genesis 2:7). He received
more than life for his body; he received spiritual life,
life in fellowship with God. But in spite of God's warning, man by his self-will and disobedience broke that
fellowship with God, and lost that life. Man, as sinner,
is still alive in his body; but the repeated statement of
the Bible is that in his spirit he is dead. He has lost that
life with God (as a child of God) for which God made
him. 'The soul that sins shall die' (Ezekiel 18:4). 'The
wages of sin is death' (Romans 6:23). You 'were dead
through . . . trespasses and sins' (verse 1), 'alienated
from the life of God' (4:18).

b. Following the world's standards

The Bible often speaks of 'this world' with a special
meaning. God made the world, and His creation shows
His power and glory. But where men rule in the world,
they often rule with little thought of God or of His will.
So the world's standards are not God's standards; the
world's ideals are not God's ideals. We often take
step after step along the road of life 'following the
course of this world' instead of following the ways of
God. (Compare Romans 12:1-2.) We love the world
and what it stands for more than we love God. (See
1 John 2:15-17.) This is our sin and our folly.

c. Obeying the evil one

The New Testament often reminds us too that there
is a spiritual power of evil. We obey God, or we obey
the one who is the enemy of all good. We are children
of God, hearing His word, or children of the devil,
accepting his temptations and persuasions (John 8:44).
Under whom do we serve? When we purposely choose

evil instead of God, the way of self-glory instead of the glory of God, we make plain who is our master. This is our sin and our folly.

d. Controlled by selfish desires

Verse 3 speaks of 'the passions of our flesh'. These include all unlawful sexual desires, but much more also. They include all our selfishness and self-will. Moreover, Paul thinks not only of our passions and emotions that can drive us and make us seek only our own enjoyment. He thinks of our minds, with which we make our plans and work out our ambitions – with *self* in the centre. This is our sin and our folly.

e. Under the judgment of God

Our sin is not only our folly, resulting in so many things that are our own great loss. Sin is offence against the holiness and love of God. God must hate sin, as it works against the best that He seeks for His creatures whom He loves. He must remove sin from His holy sight. If the sinner clings to his sin, he must know that he, by the very nature of what he is doing, is under the judgment of God, a 'child of wrath'. So Paul concludes here, as he does when he deals with the sin of man in Romans 1-3: we are all silenced before Him; we have no excuse; through our own fault we have sinned; we are all under God's judgment. But Paul will go on to say that we need not remain there. There is a way of forgiveness, deliverance and life – for all who will turn from the paths of sin to God our Saviour.

Prayer. *O Lord God, holy and righteous, Thou hast searched us and known us; and we, through our own choice, have followed the world's standards instead of Thy standards,* *evil instead of good, our selfish desires instead of Thy perfect will. We deserve only Thy righteous judgment, but grant to us, before it is too late, repentance and life, through Jesus Christ our Saviour.* AMEN.

Notes. 1. The root meanings of the words for 'trespasses' and 'sins' are 'missing the mark', and 'slipping from' or 'falling from the way'. So both speak of man's failure to live as he could do and ought to do.

2. The devil is described in verse 2 as 'the prince of the power of the air'. This does not mean that Paul supports the ancient idea that the air is full of spirits of evil. The devil is 'the ruler of this world' (John 12:31; 14:30; 16:11), but his power is not material but spiritual.

3. As in 1:12–14 we see here how Paul changes from 'you' to 'we'. He is writing to Gentile readers, but he wants to make clear to them that the Jews also (of whom he was one), though the people of God, had sinned and were under God's judgment.

Further Study. Study the use of the word 'walk' in 2:2, 10; 5:2, 8, 15 and 1 John 1:6. What do these passages say about the way in which a person may 'walk' in his daily life, and the way in which the Christian ought to take each fresh step throughout life?

Study 13. LIFE THROUGH CHRIST

'But God, who is rich in mercy, out of the great love with which he loved us, even when we were dead through our trespasses, made us alive together with Christ (by grace you have been saved), and raised us up with him, and made us

sit with him in the heavenly places in Christ Jesus' (2:4–6).

Paul's way, as we see in Romans 1–3 and Colossians 1:21–22, is to speak of God's redeeming and restoring work, only when he has made clear the terrible position and great need of man, because of sin. He has made this clear here, and so he goes on 'But God'. God breaks in. God acts in mercy. God saves. God gives new life.

a. The mercy of God

God would not leave man in his sin, although this was what he deserved. He made man for fellowship with Himself; and He is 'rich in mercy'. His glory and His greatness is His grace (1:6). There is an infinite love with which He has loved us. So He would not leave us in our sin. He must come down to rescue us.

b. The salvation of God

By that grace and love, favour that we can never deserve (see on 1:2), He has saved us from our sin. This salvation of God is the greatest subject of the New Testament. It is the Christian good news. Paul speaks of it here as the great work of God for us in Jesus Christ; he repeats himself with further explanation in verses 8 and 9. We were in a desperate condition, and could do nothing to help ourselves – but we are saved by grace. Our part is faith, accepting what God offers (see John 1:12), without pretending that we can deserve His gift. Paul knows the pride and the deceitfulness of the human heart. Sooner or later we want to suggest that God's blessings depend in some way on our deserving them. Paul rejects that, and emphasizes 'by grace', 'not your own doing, it is the gift of God', 'not because of works, lest any man should boast'.

c. The life of God

Because sin meant death, salvation means new life (see Romans 6:23). No longer – if we have faith – are we 'dead in sin'; we are 'made alive'. John's Gospel shows the quality of that life by describing it as 'eternal life'. Here it is life 'with Christ'. As Christ was raised from the dead, we too, with Him, are raised. We have life in the presence of Christ now – life 'in the heavenly places' now (see on 1:3). That means that no longer do the standards of the world rule us, the desires of the world, the aim of pleasing the world; no longer do we put first our own comforts, possessions, position, passions. We are in the world still, but we do not belong to the world (see John 17:15-16). Our citizenship is in heaven (see Philippians 3:20); our life is with Christ, new life from the dead as truly as His was when He was raised the third day after He was crucified (see Colossians 3:1-3 and Romans 12:1-2).

Prayer. *Lord of all love, Thy mercy is beyond all our thoughts, Thy salvation meets our deepest needs. Thou hast come to us in our slavery to sin, and given us new life. Help us to trust Thee completely, to glorify Thee and not ourselves, and to live daily doing Thy will as it is done in heaven.*

AMEN.

Further Study. Study the ways in which the New Testament can speak of our salvation as past, present, and future; and consider the meaning of each. See verses 5 and 8 of this chapter; 2 Timothy 1:9; 1 Corinthians 1:18; 15:2; 2 Corinthians 2:15; Romans 5:9-10; 1 Corinthians 3:15.

Study 14.
THE PURPOSE OF LIFE IN CHRIST

God has raised us up with Christ '. . . that in the coming ages he might show the immeasurable riches of his grace in kindness toward us in Christ Jesus. For by grace you have been saved through faith; and this is not your own doing, it is the gift of God – not because of works, lest any man should boast. For we are his workmanship, created in Christ Jesus for good works, which God prepared beforehand, that we should walk in them' (2:7–10).

We have seen already, in the study of 1:3–14, that Paul never stops with telling us the blessings that we can have in Christ. They are not just for us to enjoy, but also for us to share with others. If we receive new life, we have a duty and responsibility to show that new life. The knowledge of salvation is not the end, but the beginning of Christian living. What then is Christian living?

a. Showing God's grace

In 1:3–14 Paul has shown already the purpose of our blessings in Christ that we might live 'to the praise of his glorious grace'. Because our own works could not win our acceptance with God – because we have all done wrong in His sight – we can only glory in the gift of His salvation (Romans 3:27), in the cross (Galatians 6:14) and in the Saviour who suffered there for us (1 Corinthians 1:29–31 and Philippians 3:8–9). God's purpose is that we should glory in Him, and that we should show His grace. In Galatians 1: 15–16, where Paul is telling the story of his own experience of Christ, he speaks of God's grace, God's call, the revealing of

His Son Jesus Christ – and all for the purpose 'that I might preach him among the Gentiles'. We have received the knowledge of that same grace, that we might pass it on to others. But here Paul's vision of our showing this grace reaches beyond this world to 'the coming ages'. Not only now and in this world, but far beyond, we who are saved by the grace of Christ's cross will be living examples of the kindness and mercy of God. (See also 3:10.)

b. Showing good works

Paul's vision reaches to distant worlds and to the far future, but in verse 10 he is back to life here and now. 'Works' cannot be our way of salvation, but our salvation must be worked out in life (see Philippians 2:12). It must lead to good works. Salvation means new life; or, as verse 10 puts it, it is a new creation by God. (See 2 Corinthians 5:17; Galatians 6:15; Colossians 3:10.) And the very purpose of this creation is 'good works'. We must question whether we have God's salvation, if there is no fruit of good works in our lives. There are also particular good works that He has in His plan for each of our lives, a particular way for us to walk in, step by step, when once we have turned round from the walk 'following the course of this world' (verse 2). In this, His way, God seeks to lead us, that by our 'good works' we may glorify Him (see Matthew 5:16).

Prayer. *Lord God, in Thy Mercy Thou hast saved us and created us anew in Christ; lead and strengthen us that by our good works others may be blessed and Thy name honoured.* AMEN.

Further Study. Compare Paul's teaching here and in other places, that salvation is not by works but leading to good works, with the teaching of James 2:14–26.

2:11–22. THE WAY OF PEACE THROUGH CHRIST

PAUL HAS spoken of the gift of new life for those who were dead in sin. Now he has another way to describe what God has done. He has not only reconciled sinful men so that they are at peace with Him; He has also brought them to be at peace one with another. He has broken down barriers of hatred and pride. He has broken down racial divisions.

Study 15.
THOSE FAR FROM GOD BROUGHT NEAR

'Therefore remember that at one time you Gentiles in the flesh, called the uncircumcision by what is called the circumcision, which is made in the flesh by hands – remember that you were at that time separated from Christ, alienated from the commonwealth of Israel, and strangers to the covenants of promise, having no hope and without God in the world. But now in Christ Jesus you who once were far off have been brought near in the blood of Christ' (2:11–13).

Paul was a Jew, brought up in the faith of one God, and the hope of the coming Christ; but from the time of his conversion, he had felt called to go out to those who were not Jews, the Gentiles (Acts 9:15). He knew that his own Jewish people were as much in need of Christ as any, but he always marvelled at God's way

49

of bringing the Gentiles who were far from Him to be near to Him.

a. They were outside God's people

The Jews boasted in religious privileges that the Gentiles did not have. In particular the Jews had the covenant with God, of which circumcision was the outward sign. Paul, like the prophets and the law in Old Testament days, said that the custom of circumcision had no religious value if it was only outward, and if there was no faith or obedience in people's lives (see Romans 2:25–29). Yet the fact remained that the Gentiles were in the past 'strangers to the covenants of promise'; they were 'alienated from the commonwealth of Israel', that is, they did not belong among the people through whom God was working out His special purpose for the world (see Romans 3:1–2; 9:4–5).

b. They were without hope

The Old Testament is a book of hope and of promise. It is always pointing forward. From the days of Abraham the people of Israel had a promise and a hope. They were not intended to keep that hope selfishly for themselves. God wanted them to bring the blessing of their knowledge of Him to all nations (Genesis 12:3), to be a light to the Gentiles (Isaiah 42:1, 6; 49:6). In fact they did this very little. The Gentiles were for the most part 'separated from Christ', and in the days when Christ came the Greeks and Romans of Paul's world were people without hope. The Greeks had the idea of history going round and round in great circles without a goal. Today the heathen world, and the world in which only material things matter, is a world without hope. Funeral customs frequently show this most clearly – there we see the great difference between those who sorrow without hope, and those whose faith and hope it is that the gift of God through Christ is eternal life, life victorious over death (see 1 Thessalonians 4:13).

c. They were without God

There were many 'gods' and many 'lords' in the world of the apostles (1 Corinthians 8:5), but the knowledge of the one true God and Lord over all was lacking. The gods whom they worshipped were no gods (Galatians 4:8). The crowds to whom Paul preached in one country after another were 'without God in the world'. They faced the world with all its problems and uncertainties, all its fears and trials, all its sorrows and suffering, without God.

It was not God's will that the world should be so. But Paul, as a Pharisee, seems to have done little for Gentiles. Now, however, life had become different for him. Jesus was the Christ. He, the Son of God, had come because God so loved the *world*. Speaking of His death on the cross, He said, 'I, when I am lifted up from the earth, will draw all men to myself' – Gentiles as well as Jews, He meant. (See John 3:16 and 12:20–24, 32.) Those outside God's people and without hope, those far off, are 'brought near in the blood of Christ'. Paul, with heart and soul, with all his time and strength, was a messenger of that glorious gospel. All of us who know the gospel as Paul did, are to take it to those who today are people 'having no hope and without God in the world'.

Prayer. *Lord, may we, to whom Thou hast given life and hope and all things, so live in this world as Thy people, that*

*through us those who do not know Thee may come near to Thee,
rest in Thee, and serve Thee for ever.* AMEN.

Further Study. Study the following passages that
show how circumcision was the outward sign of Israel's
covenant with God, but that it was of no value if it was
only outward, and not accompanied by faith and
obedience in a person's life: Genesis 17:1-12; Deuteronomy 10:16; Jeremiah 9:26; Romans 2:25-29; 1
Corinthians 7:19; Galatians 5:6; 6:15. Can a similar
principle apply to the Christian sacraments without
faith and obedience?

Study 16. THE WAY OF PEACE

**'For he is our peace, who has made us both one,
and has broken down the dividing wall of hostility, by abolishing in his flesh the law of commandments and ordinances, that he might
create in himself one new man in place of the
two, so making peace, and might reconcile us
both to God in one body through the cross,
thereby bringing the hostility to an end. And he
came and preached peace to you who were far
off and peace to those who were near; for through
him we both have access in one Spirit to the
Father'** (2:14-18).

In verses 1-10 Paul has described the work of Christ
as bringing life to the dead; in verses 11-13 he shows
how those far off have been brought near. God's
gift of peace is the subject of these next five verses.

a. Peace with God

Sin makes us all enemies of God. We are men and

women working against His loving and perfect purpose, instead of living the life for which He made us, in fellowship with Him. We have caused strife, and have rebelled against our Maker. Our greatest need is reconciliation. That need is met in Christ. God has reconciled us to Himself by Christ, and He has done this 'through the cross'. Because Christ died, we have forgiveness of our sins. Because Christ was slain there, the hostility of our rebellion is slain. (2 Corinthians 5:18–21 and 1 Peter 2:24 express this truth.) Christ is our Peace. As we are 'in him' we have peace. We are no longer enemies, but as friends of God and children of God we have 'access . . . to the Father'.

b. The way of peace for all

This way of peace is the only way. The Jew needs it – in one sense he was near before because of his knowledge of God and his hope of the Christ; but because of his rebellion he was far away. The Gentile needs it – he is far away from God, both because of his ignorance and his rebellion even against the best he knows. Both have peace and access to God in the same way, the only way. It is the one way still, the same for 'civilized' and 'uncivilized', for young and old, for men and women, for educated and uneducated, for the mighty and the lowly (see Romans 1:14–16; Acts 26:29).

c. Peace one with another

If there is one way of life and peace for people of different races, classes and colours, it follows that there is a bond of unity between them that did not exist before; and no earthly society can provide a stronger bond. In particular, there was before a mighty barrier between Jews and Gentiles. In the Temple in Jerusalem there was a stone wall, and on it a notice forbidding any Gentile to enter – and the penalty was death. The door of every Jewish home was closed to Gentiles, and a Gentile could not go into the house of a Jew or eat with him (see Acts 11:2–3). If a Jew married a Gentile, he was treated as if he had died. The Jew had the law with all its detailed ordinances, and because the Gentile did not keep this law, Jew and Gentile could not live together. Now the way to God is open for all – not by the law, but by faith in Jesus Christ. It is the same for Jew and non-Jew. They come 'to God in one body'. Peace with God, and peace one with another, is the result. In Christ there is a new fellowship between man and man, as well as between man and God. To every Christian Paul can say, 'There is neither Jew nor Greek, there is neither slave nor free, there is neither male nor female; for you are all one in Christ Jesus' (Galatians 3:28). In that fellowship of Christ's family (as nowhere else) the barrier between Jew and Gentile is down, and every other barrier too. We are one before God; we have one way to God; by faith we come into the one body, which is His church; and together we will live with Him for ever.

Prayer. *Lord, we praise Thee that Thou art bringing into one family men and women out of every tribe and nation. Use us in this Thy work. Give us love for all people, and take from our hearts all pride. So may we know and keep the unity of the Spirit in the bond of peace, through Jesus Christ the Saviour and Lord of us all.* AMEN.

Notes. 1. The law was a cause of distinction and hostility between Jews and Gentiles (verse 15), especially in the way that it had many ceremonial rules (such as those of clean and unclean meats); those who did not keep these rules were despised and cut off by all strict Jews.

2. Verse 17 quotes Isaiah 57:19 and probably also Isaiah 52:7. This is why the verse speaks of the preaching of peace. The main point is, not when Christ thus preached peace, before or after His resurrection, but that He came 'with a gospel of peace'.

Further Study. 1. Consider how the Old Testament hope was of the bringing of peace – *e.g.* Isaiah 9:6-7; 53:5 (AV); Micah 5:5; Haggai 2:9 (AV); Zechariah 9:10; and how the New Testament tells of Christ bringing peace – *e.g.* Luke 1:79; 2:14; Acts 10:36; Romans 5:1; Colossians 1:20.

2. Read Acts 10 to see the way that Peter had to learn the truth of these verses.

Study 17. NEW PRIVILEGES OF POSITION

'So then you are no longer strangers and sojourners, but you are fellow citizens with the saints and members of the household of God, built upon the foundation of the apostles and prophets, Christ Jesus himself being the chief cornerstone, in whom the whole structure is joined together and grows into a holy temple in the Lord; in whom you also are built into it for a dwelling place of God in the Spirit' (2:19-22).

There has come to be life where there was death in sin before. There is peace where there was war and rebellion, man against God. Before there were no rights and privileges. Men, separate from Christ, were 'alienated from the commonwealth of Israel, and strangers to the covenants of promise'; they had 'no

55

hope' and were 'without God in the world'. Now all is different.

a. We are the people of God

No longer are we 'strangers and sojourners', those who live in a country but without any of the rights and privileges of citizenship. The Epistle to the Hebrews (11:13 and 13:14) says that men of faith are always like this in the world. 'For here we have no lasting city.' But we are members of God's people, with all the privileges that such membership brings. God is our God and He will never leave us. We are 'fellow citizens with the saints'. That is, we belong together with all those who have served God down the ages – with Abraham and Moses, David and the prophets, the apostles and all faithful Christians of every race and colour and of every age. We stand in a great fellowship; the Lord whom all these served and found faithful is our Lord. We are His people.

b. We are the family of God

We are closer to God than a nation to its ruler. We are 'the household of God', because we are members of 'the household of faith' (Galatians 6:10). We are more than the people of God, we are 'children of God' (John 1:12), and we come to Him as our Father. (See on 1:5.) These words thus show our relationship to Him, and the meaning of prayer – as a child's confident approach to his father. They also show our relationship to our fellow-Christians. Whatever our tribe or nation or class, we are brothers and sisters; and we should notice how frequently the New Testament speaks of Christians as the 'brethren'.

c. We are the building of God

The church is like the household or family of God. It is also like a house, a building which has a firm foundation. In 1 Corinthians 3:11 Paul speaks of Christ as the Foundation. Here he speaks of the apostles and prophets, those who first preached the gospel, as part of the foundation. (See Matthew 16:16–18.) Christ is the Corner-stone of that foundation, the most important part of all. Into Him all the rest have to fit – apostles and prophets, and those who are added to them in the building. We are in the church, the building of God, if we build our lives on the teaching that the apostles received from Christ Himself. Above all, we have our place as we are rightly related to Christ, the Corner-stone. He gives direction to the whole building, and indicates the place that each stone should have in it.

d. We are the temple of God

It might seem a deeper truth about the church to describe it as a family than as a building. Certainly to describe the church as a building is not to express the whole truth about it. It is rather like a building that has life in it, a building that grows of itself. (See 1 Peter 2:5.) But Paul wants most to liken it to a building in which God Himself lives. In the Old Testament the Temple was not just a place of worship for the Jews; it was the place in which God's presence was specially known (2 Chronicles 5:13–14 and 7:1–3). There is no temple now like that which the Jews had. Paul says to us, 'You are God's temple, and . . . God's Spirit dwells in you' (see 1 Corinthians 3:16 and 6:19, and 2 Corinthians 6:16) – 'you also are built . . . for a dwelling place of God in the Spirit.' We must therefore allow no evil nor any strife to come into the temple of our body; in

57

our personal lives and in our fellowship one with another we are to show the glory and grace and power of His presence.

Prayer. *O God, our Almighty Creator and Lord, we praise Thee for the great privileges that we have in Christ; may we live in the world, showing forth Thy presence, that we may be known by others as Thy people who serve Thee, and Thy children who know Thee as Father, through Jesus Christ our Saviour.* AMEN.

Notes. 1. In verse 20 the 'prophets' are those of the New Testament and not of the Old Testament. This is clear from the order here, and from the context. In 4:11 Paul says more about these Christian prophets (see notes below on that verse).

2. Psalm 118:22 (quoted in Mark 12:10; Acts 4:11, and 1 Peter 2:7) gives us the thought of Christ as the Corner-stone. See also Isaiah 28:16.

3. In verse 21 the reference is not to many buildings, but to many parts of one building.

Further Study. See what the New Testament has to say about the fulfilment of the meaning of the temple – in John 2:19-20; Acts 7:48; 1 Corinthians 3:16-17; 6:19; 2 Corinthians 6:16; Revelation 3:12; 7:15; 11:19.

3:1–13. THE PRIVILEGE OF CHRISTIAN PREACHING

IN CHAPTERS 1 and 2 Paul has spoken of the rich blessings that there are in Christ, and especially of the difference that they have made to Gentiles who previously were without any knowledge of God, without any hope. As apostle to the Gentiles, he wants to go on to pray for them, that they may know fully the power and wisdom and love of God in Christ. He is about to say, 'For this reason I bow my knees' (verse 14); but he cannot help stopping to speak of his own position and privilege before he prays. He does so, not to exalt himself, but to praise further the grace of God.

Study 18. PAUL, THE PRISONER

'For this reason I, Paul, a prisoner for Christ Jesus on behalf of you Gentiles' (3:1).

'Paul, an apostle of Christ Jesus by the will of God' are the words of 1:1. Now this apostle has something different to say about himself.

a. He is a prisoner

As he wrote this letter, Paul was a Roman prisoner. He may have been free to be in his own hired house (see Acts 28:30, margin); but he was chained to a Roman soldier (6:20). This great servant of Christ who had travelled to many lands and nations, and preached the gospel to untold thousands, was able to move no more than a goat tied to a post. Even so he does not complain, nor pity himself. He does not speak of himself as a prisoner so that others may feel sympathy for him. Rather he wants them to rejoice and praise God (verse 13). He himself could rejoice and feel content, even with his chains (see Philippians 4:4, 11–13).

b. He is a prisoner of Christ Jesus

Paul thought less of the chains that bound him to the Roman soldier than of the unseen chains that bound him to Jesus Christ. Paul knew the power of Christ, his Master. If He wished, He could break those Roman chains, as He did for him in Philippi, and for Peter in Jerusalem (Acts 16:26 and 12:7). If He did not wish this, then Paul was 'a prisoner for Christ Jesus', content with His purpose. In prison the presence and power and grace of Christ did not fail him and would not fail him. If he could not witness to the many, he could show Christ to the few who came to him. He could pray, and no-one could bind those prayers. He could write, and those letters of his have been let loose on the world, and have brought freedom and peace and eternal life to many from one end of the earth to the other. Do we realize what we can do for God, even though we may be limited by circumstances, by difficulties or by weakness?

c. He is a prisoner for the sake of the Gentiles

Paul was a prisoner because he had preached the gospel. More particularly he was a prisoner because he had given himself to preach the gospel to the Gentiles. In Jerusalem the Jews so bitterly opposed him, and caused his imprisonment, because he declared that the door to the kingdom of God was open to the Gentiles. They said that he brought Greeks into the Temple, and in particular they thought that he had taken Trophimus the Ephesian into God's house (Acts 21:28-29). Because of what he had done for the Gentiles, Paul was imprisoned. But for the sake of the blessing it could be to Gentiles, Paul continued to remain (in the perfect will of God) in prison. Gentile Christians did not need to say with discouragement, 'Our great apostle is in prison' (see verse 13). Rather they could find encouragement and gain courage every time they remembered, 'Our great apostle is willing to suffer all this for Christ; should we not be bold to witness to our Lord?' (see Philippians 1:14).

Prayer. *Christ Jesus, our unchanging Lord, in Thy power be near to all who now are suffering imprisonment or persecution for Thy sake. When we face discouragement or trial, help us to remain faithful, to rejoice and to pray, so that our difficulties may be a means that Thou canst use to strengthen and bless others; for Thy name's sake.* AMEN.

Further Study. Find out which of Paul's letters were written from prison, and so consider the work that he was able to do at the time of imprisonment, both among those who came to him, and through his letters.

Study 19.
PAUL, APOSTLE TO THE GENTILES

'Assuming that you have heard of the steward-ship of God's grace that was given to me for you, how the mystery was made known to me by revelation, as I have written briefly. When you

read this you can perceive my insight into the mystery of Christ, which was not made known to the sons of men in other generations as it has now been revealed to his holy apostles and prophets by the Spirit; that is, how the Gentiles are fellow heirs, members of the same body, and partakers of the promise in Christ Jesus through the gospel. Of this gospel I was made a minister according to the gift of God's grace which was given me by the working of his power' (3:2-7).

In verse 1 Paul has described himself as a prisoner for the sake of the Gentiles. In fact his whole life was given to the work of preaching the gospel to the Gentiles. Two great changes had taken place at the time of Paul's conversion. The persecutor of the Christians had become a servant of Christ; but also his whole attitude to those who were not Jews became completely different. He had been a Jew of the strictest sect of the Pharisees (Acts 26:5); it would have been much harder for him than for Peter to go and eat in the house of a Gentile. After his conversion he came to live far more among Gentiles than among his own people. The things that he would have thought absolutely impossible before, he now came to see as the greatest possible God-given privilege.

a. The privilege of God's call

He had been separated from the Gentiles by a barrier that he could not pass, and did not wish to pass. Now he realized that it was his greatest privilege to go to the Gentiles, and preach to them 'the unsearchable riches of Christ' (verse 8). In verse 2 he speaks of 'the stewardship of God's grace that was given' to him; that was the work which God in His love had given to him, that he should be the apostle of the Gentiles. From the depth of his heart he thanked God that this was his calling and that God gave him power also to serve in this way (verse 7).

b. The privilege of God's truth

Before his conversion he had acted in ignorance – towards Christ, towards the Christians, towards Gentiles. Now he knew the truth. 'When you read this', he said, 'you can perceive my insight into the mystery of Christ'; and he did not say this proudly. He did not understand before God opened his eyes to see. He had only what God had revealed to him 'in the Spirit'. In earlier generations, even in the Old Testament, men only understood a part of the truth. Now, in His amazing grace, God has shown the truth to His apostles and His prophets, and through them to all who are willing to receive it. The 'mystery', the revealed truth (see on 1:9), is the gospel itself. It is also the fact that the gospel is for all – its blessings are for all fully to share in, of whatever race they are.

c. The privilege of God's inheritance

In verse 6 Paul describes in three ways the blessings which Jews and Gentiles share equally in Christ. First, they have God's inheritance. The riches of God's house and of God's family belong to them – eternal life and peace and joy and freedom, the knowledge of the Father and of His work in the universe that He has made. Secondly, they are members of the body of Christ – their life is joined to His life; His work is their work; He, as Head, directs and inspires them. Thirdly, they have His promise, that what they do not possess fully now they will possess when they see Him face to face.

All these things are ours too, on the same condition. We must only be willing to receive them, and that willingness is faith.

Prayer. *Lord, fill our hearts with praise that Thy gospel is for all people. Fill us with zeal and power to show Thy gospel to all whom we can reach. Give us grace to learn all the truth Thou hast for us, and to possess all the blessings Thou hast for us. And may it be our joy to serve Thee to Thy praise and glory, now and for ever.* AMEN.

Notes. 1. Verse 2 is another indication that this letter was written not only for the church of Ephesus, but for a number of churches. In Ephesus they would have known Paul well as the apostle of the Gentiles; in other places they would not have been so familiar with God's special call to him.

2. In verse 5, as in 2:20, the prophets are obviously those of the Christian church and not of the Old Testament. (See on 4:11.)

Further Study. Study with this section what Galatians 1:11–23 and 2:1–16 teach about Paul's calling as apostle to the Gentiles, and the way that he presented the gospel as the same for both Jews and Gentiles.

Study 20.
THE GLORY OF THE APOSTLE'S MESSAGE

'To me, though I am the very least of all the saints, this grace was given, to preach to the Gentiles the unsearchable riches of Christ, and to make all men see what is the plan of the mystery hidden for ages in God who created all things; that through the church the manifold

wisdom of God might now be made known to the principalities and powers in the heavenly places. This was according to the eternal purpose which he has realized in Christ Jesus our Lord, in whom we have boldness and confidence of access through our faith in him. So I ask you not to lose heart over what I am suffering for you, which is your glory' (3:8-13).

As Paul thought of his work as an apostle, and as he tried to encourage the Christians to whom he was writing, he used words that speak of the glory of the gospel and the great privilege of the messenger of the gospel. We can best study verses 8-13 by thinking especially of four phrases that he used.

a. Unsearchable riches

It was not just the 'gospel' that Paul had to preach, but Christ. The gospel is Christ. (See 1 Corinthians 2:2.) We are to tell the world the unsearchable riches of Christ. Jesus, in His parables, said that the kingdom of heaven is like a 'pearl of great value', or like treasure which it is worth a person giving up all that he has to possess (Matthew 13:44-46). There is no end of the riches of Christ. He 'bestows his riches upon all who call upon him' (Romans 10:12). He is rich to meet every need we have. We can go on learning His riches in our minds and proving them in our experience; we can go on all our days, and there will still be an abundance of His love and goodness and wisdom that we have not learnt at the end.

b. Manifold wisdom

His wisdom is rich beyond anything that we can

even think. In Colossians 2:3 Paul says that in Christ 'are hid all the treasures of wisdom and knowledge'. Here he speaks of the 'manifold wisdom of God', and he uses a word that was used to describe many-coloured flowers or cloth. How wise is our God in so many ways! We can think of the wisdom of His creation, the wisdom of the way He chose to redeem mankind, and the wisdom He has shown in bringing each of us to Himself. We can learn this wisdom, but it is also our work to tell it to others – as Paul puts it in verse 9, to bring all people to see the plan of God concerning the truth that has been hidden in past ages but now is revealed. Our work of showing His wisdom, however, is not just in the present and in this world. The church can even tell the powers in heaven things that they have never known about God's wisdom. (See 1 Peter 1:12.) They have known God's wisdom in creation and in ruling this universe but, as the hymn puts it, 'They have never, never known, a fallen world like this.' So they have never known the grace of His forgiveness, and the wisdom of His plan for man's salvation. As we praise Him for this, we can add to His glory, even in heaven.

c. Eternal purpose

So God has a plan and purpose for man that is not just of the present world. It reaches heaven, and it also goes on to all eternity. It reaches right back into the past. In the Bible we see God's plan for our salvation being worked out back in the days of Abraham, in the time of Moses, in the time of David, and through all the prophets. It goes back further than any of these – to the heart and mind of God. So it is an eternal purpose. 'Before the foundation of the world' (1:4) God chose us to be His people, holy and without blemish. He wants us to be His people for ever and ever. He has laid hold of us; He will not let us go.

d. The very least of all the saints

Who are we, that we should know and tell the unsearchable riches of Christ, the manifold wisdom, the eternal purpose of God? The very least important, least likely, least worthy of all. Paul a persecutor, a few simple fishermen, a tax-collector – He chose people like these at first; and now He chooses people like us. We are not worthy, and yet He has taken us. If such is His grace and love, we need fear nothing. 'Jesus we know, and He is on the throne.' We have 'access' to His throne of grace (see Hebrews 4:16). We have His strength, and so we have boldness in the world. We do not need to faint nor become discouraged, whatever our difficulties may be. His eternal purpose is worth living for, worth suffering for, worth dying for; His unsearchable riches are worth passing on to all who do not know Him.

Prayer. *Lord, Thou hast called us to share in Thy eternal purpose, help us to grow daily in Thy manifold wisdom, and make us glad and bold witnesses to the unsearchable riches of Thy Son Jesus Christ.* AMEN.

Further Study. Study the use of the word 'boldness' or 'confidence' in the New Testament, describing the freedom the Christian has in coming to God, and also his courage among men. See especially Acts 4:13, 29, 31; Philippians 1:20; Hebrews 10:19; 1 John 2:28; 3:21; 4:17; 5:14.

3:14–21. PRAYER FOR STRENGTH, WISDOM AND LOVE

WE HAVE followed one of the great prayers of the apostle in the second part of chapter 1. Here is another prayer, and again Paul asks from God the greatest possible spiritual blessings for his readers.

Study 21. TO PRAYER AGAIN

'For this reason I bow my knees before the Father, from whom every family in heaven and on earth is named, that according to the riches of his glory he may grant you to be strengthened with might through his Spirit in the inner man' (3:14–16a).

As was the case with that earlier prayer in chapter 1, so from this prayer, too, we can learn many things for our own praying.

a. The reason for prayer

We saw as we studied verse 1 that Paul was beginning to pray there, and began 'for this reason', but he felt he must say more of what it meant to him to be 'a prisoner for Christ Jesus on behalf of . . . Gentiles'. Now he returns to the point at which he broke off – 'for this reason I pray', he is going to say. For what reason? He has thought of how those who were dead in sin have been brought to life in Christ, of how those who were far off have been brought near. They have come into the people of God, into the building of God, and are to be 'a dwelling place of God in the Spirit'. These people, then, greatly need the apostle's prayers, that they may be able 'to lead a life worthy of the calling' to which they are called (4:1). In what he has said from verse 1 onwards, he has added to the reasons for his prayer. He is their apostle, with great responsibility towards them; and they are in danger of fainting and being discouraged because of their difficulties. So Paul prays; and for similar reasons we should pray, for ourselves and for others – realizing the greatness of our blessings, our needs, our privileges, our responsibilities.

b. The Father who hears prayer

Paul prays like this because he knows the God who hears prayer. He is 'the Father', and to Him the Christian can come freely, because he comes through the Son (see 2:18–19). Once again (compare 1:17) Paul cannot just use this name, and leave it. He is 'the Father, from whom every family in heaven and on earth is named'. All the best that we know of fatherhood comes from Him. One early Christian writer put it, 'The name of father did not go up from us, but from above it came to us.' It is to the perfect Father that we come when we pray. 'As a father pities his children, so the Lord pities those who fear him' (Psalm 103:13; and see also Matthew 7:11).

c. The riches of His answers to prayer

We can approach Him as children come to their father; but He is the almighty Father. He gives 'according to the riches of his glory'. Paul has already

brought us to think several times of the 'riches' of God
(1:7, 18; 2:4, 7; 3:8), far far greater than all the riches
of earth. Out of these riches He gives to those who
pray to Him, but not only out of the riches but 'according to them'. As great as His riches are, so greatly and
freely He gives. Furthermore the 'riches' are 'riches of
his glory'. His glory is His greatness; it is the greatness
of His love and grace and mercy (1:6). His glory is to
love us, to seek what is best for us, to give His highest
gifts to us. To such a Father we come, knowing that He
wants to give to us 'according to the riches of his glory'.

d. The attitude for prayer

Paul knew he could come freely to his heavenly
Father. He knew His desire to give and give and give
to His children. Nevertheless he came humbly and
earnestly. 'I bow my knees', he said. The Bible tells
us of many ways in which people pray to God – sitting,
standing, raising the hands up to heaven. Kneeling,
which has rightly come to be the general way for
Christians' praying, expresses the deepest earnestness.
So Solomon prayed when the Temple was dedicated
(1 Kings 8:54), Stephen when he was dying (Acts
7:60), Peter when he prayed for Dorcas (Acts 9:40),
Paul when he was farewelled on the way to Jerusalem
(Acts 20:36 and 21:5). Above all, Christ knelt to pray in
Gethsemane before He suffered (Luke 22:41). We can
pray to God with the greatest freedom, but we should
never forget how earnest our prayer should be; and
Ecclesiastes 5:2 still applies to us, when it says, Remember that 'God is in heaven, and you upon earth'.

Prayer. *God Almighty, King of kings, and Lord of lords,
our Creator and our Judge, we praise Thee that we can come
to Thee as Father, and as the God of all grace. Teach us how*

*to pray. May our privileges lead us to come to Thee humbly
and thankfully. And may the needs of others lead us to be men
and women who live lives of prayer; through the strength of
Christ our Saviour.* AMEN.

Further Study. In what ways does the Bible speak of
God as Father? See especially 1:3; Romans 15:6; John
10:38; Acts 17:28–29; Hebrews 12:9; Exodus 4:22–23;
Isaiah 1:2; John 14:6; Galatians 3:26; 4:6, *etc.*

Study 22. SUBJECTS FOR PRAYER

**I pray that you may 'be strengthened with might
through his Spirit in the inner man, and that
Christ may dwell in your hearts through faith;
that you, being rooted and grounded in love, may
have power to comprehend with all the saints
what is the breadth and length and height and
depth, and to know the love of Christ which
surpasses knowledge, that you may be filled
with all the fullness of God'** (3:16b–19).

It is necessary to take all these petitions of Paul's
great prayer together, as they belong so closely; but
each one deserves close study and deep meditation.

a. Strength

Paul thinks of the needs and temptations of the
Christians to whom he writes, and he prays that they
may know the strength of God. As in 1:19 and in 6:10
he is not satisfied with one word to describe it, but asks
that they may 'be strengthened with might' (see also
Colossians 1:11). By the power of the Spirit of Christ
they would be made able to do anything (see Philippians

4:13). For this power does not just come from outside. It is a strength that the Christian can have deep down in his inner life, and so he is able with it to meet every danger and trial and disappointment that comes. Outside the storms may blow; from within there is strength to resist the fiercest storm.

b. Christ indwelling

To Paul the 'Spirit in the inner man' is the same as saying 'Christ in you' (see Romans 8:9–10). He is not only with us, He is in us. So we have not only strength in us, but also the *Source* of strength and comfort, wisdom and love. We have Christ in us, if we have faith, because faith means that our lives are joined to Christ. Faith means that we invite Christ to come in and rule our lives (see John 1:12 and Revelation 3:20).

c. Rooted and grounded in love

If Christ is in us, and rules in our lives, then we rule no longer. We do not seek our own way, but Christ's. Because Christ is perfect love, our own lives are loving – they are 'rooted and grounded in love'. Love is the foundation, and so the life must be built of acts and words and thoughts of love. The roots of the life go down into love, and so the fruit must be love. In other words, if our lives are 'in Christ' in the way of which Paul so often speaks, then we must know more and more that 'love of Christ which surpasses knowledge'. And you cannot know love just in your mind – you have it in your heart, at the very centre of your self, and you express it in your life, or you do not know it at all.

d. Understanding

Paul prays also for the kind of knowledge or under-

standing that leads to loving action. The prayer for
wisdom is a great prayer. We have seen it already in
1:17-18. In these days we can go on all our lives
learning things about God's world in which we live,
and even in a life-time we can learn only a small part
of all there is to know. Yet it is far more wonderful to
know God – 'the breadth and length and height and
depth'. But Paul says that that knowledge does not just
come to us as we sit down to use our minds. It comes to
us as we are willing to have love in our lives. This is
true for two reasons. The first is that 'God is love', and
the person who is not willing to give love a place in his
life cannot know God (1 John 4:7-8). God's purpose is
a purpose of perfect love; you cannot know it if love is
shut out from your mind, just as you could not know
anything about beautiful colours if, from your birth,
light had never come into your eyes. Secondly, we
understand God 'with all the saints', that is, with all
our fellow Christians. They help us to understand, by
what they in their experience have learnt of God and of
His ways. If we depend only on ourselves, our knowledge
of God will be very weak and poor. When we love
others and share with them, we learn from them the
deep things of God.

e. The fullness of God

It is not enough for Paul to pray that we may have
the power of God, the love of God, and the wisdom of
God in us, filling us. He prays that we might 'be filled
with all the fullness of God'. Can the fullness of God
possibly be contained in one weak object of His
creation? In one way it is true to say that 'heaven and
the highest heaven cannot contain' Him – much less
any earthly house, or any human life (1 Kings 8:27).
What Paul means is that he prays for himself and for

others that no single thing of all the fullness of blessing may be lacking in the lives of those who belong to Him – no single thing of all that His presence can be in us and can do through us.

No **Prayer** can be given except Paul's prayer in these verses. Try to use it, very slowly and thoughtfully, as a prayer for yourself and for others.

Notes. 1. The word used for 'dwell' in verse 17 means a permanent rather than a temporary dwelling.

2. When Paul wrote, he knew particularly the danger of people thinking that religion was chiefly a matter of knowing things with the mind. See 1 Corinthians 1:22; Colossians 2:18, 23 and 1 Timothy 6:3-4. So Paul here, and in all his Epistles, emphasizes that faith means more than believing with the mind; it means obeying God and living a love-filled life.

Further Study. Study the following passages to see what they mean when they speak of 'the fullness of God' or 'the fullness of Christ': 1:23; 4:13; John 1:16; Colossians 1:19; 2:9.

Study 23. ALL PRAISE TO HIM WHO ANSWERS PRAYER

'**Now to him who by the power at work within us is able to do far more abundantly than all that we ask or think, to him be glory in the church and in Christ Jesus to all generations, for ever and ever. Amen**' (3:20-21).

Often Paul speaks in praise of God before he begins to pray – so he has done in chapter 1. Sometimes, as here, his petitions lead to worship, as he thinks of the

God to whom he can make such requests. Confidence and praise are the twin thoughts of these verses.

a. Confidence

Paul has made tremendous requests in the prayer he has just offered – for the power of the Spirit, the indwelling of Christ Himself, knowledge and love. He has prayed for no less a thing than that his readers might 'be filled with all the fullness of God'. What a prayer to make! And yet he knew that he could make it with confidence. He to whom we pray 'is able'. Paul loved to think of the infinite ability of God. He is able to do what we ask, when we ask things that are in accordance with His wonderful purpose for mankind. He is able to do 'far more abundantly than all that we *ask*'. More than that. His thoughts are higher and greater than our thoughts. His love is higher and greater than we can ever understand (see Isaiah 55:8–9). So He is able to give, and will give, far more abundantly than all that we can even *think*.

The apostle adds, 'by the power at work within us'. Does this take away the benefit of all he has said, because we know that His power does not work in us like this? No, His power does work in us, and will work in us, if only we let His Spirit come in. These words are in fact a further assurance. As we have seen, it means far more to know that the power of God is not just applied to our lives from outside; it is in us to work there mightily, to overcome all our weaknesses, our disappointments, our temptations, our fears. 'He who is in you is greater than he who is in the world' (1 John 4:4). He is infinitely greater, and that is our confidence.

b. Praise

Because of God's infinite power and love of which

75

Paul is so confident, he is full of praise. 'To him be glory.' It is one of the deepest and most constant temptations of the Christian to take glory to himself. We receive such rich blessings; we are lifted up with joy; we begin to think that our victories are ours, and the strength is ours; we forget that all that we have comes from our Lord alone (see Deuteronomy 8:11–18). To Him alone is the glory, and each day we must confess, 'Not to us, O Lord, not to us, but to thy name give glory' (Psalm 115:1).

To Him there is to be glory 'in the church'. In the fellowship of Christians He alone is to be exalted and praised. We who are His are to let our lights so shine that men may glorify our Father in heaven (Matthew 5:16). Above all, the glory is 'in Christ Jesus'. Our greatest work is to exalt Him whom the Father has sent to be the Saviour of the world, and who is Lord of all. Giving glory to Him is our work now, and it will be our work in the eternity to come. We will never be able to tell enough of His grace, His power, His love, and the wonder of all His works.

Prayer. *Lord God Almighty, to Thee all praise and honour is due, in the church which Thou hast chosen to fulfil Thy purposes, and in Jesus Christ Thy perfect Son our Saviour. Whatever we do, may we not think of our own praise, but Thy greatness, Thy glory, for to Thee alone all majesty, power and dominion belong, now and for ever and ever.* AMEN.

Further Study. Compare these verses with what is said about the power and the glory of God in other New Testament doxologies in Romans 11:33–36; 16:25–27; 1 Timothy 1:17; 6:15–16; Hebrews 13:20–21; Jude 24–25; Revelation 4:11; 5:12–14.

4:1–6. THE SPIRIT'S UNITY IN THE CHURCH

IN CHAPTERS 1–3 the apostle has said a great deal about the calling of the Christian, and the privileges and blessings that he has in Christ. His praise and prayer rise up to God at the thought of these. Now he goes on to speak especially of how the Christian ought to live because of this high calling. First he speaks of the humility which should be shown by each Christian. And from this he goes on to speak of the unity of the church, with all its members, with their different gifts, working together in love.

Study 24. A PRISONER'S APPEAL

'I therefore, a prisoner for the Lord, beg you to lead a life worthy of the calling to which you have been called, with all lowliness and meekness, with patience, forbearing one another in love, eager to maintain the unity of the Spirit in the bond of peace' (4:1–3).

Here, as often in Paul's letters, we have the word 'therefore', which makes us think back to what has gone before. He has said many things about the 'calling' of the Christian. He is called to know God in Jesus Christ, to know His grace, to be a child of God, to be one of His own people, to inherit His kingdom, to be a messenger of the unsearchable riches of Christ, to lay hold on the love and power and wisdom of God through prayer. Paul is saying, 'Think of this high calling, and live in a way that is worthy of it.' He says, 'I Paul, the prisoner, appeal to you to do so.' He does not remind them that he is a prisoner so as to make them pity him (see notes on 3:1). He wants rather to remind them that he does not regret having to suffer imprisonment or anything else for Christ's sake. He wants them to be willing to do anything for Christ, to follow wherever His call leads them, and to show in a worthy way that they are people whom God has called. But how must Christians live if they are to live worthily? A life like this will be seen in the quality of their personal life, and in the quality of their life together as a fellowship.

a. Qualities of personal life

The first of these is *lowliness* or humility, the opposite of self-centredness and pride. The non-Christian world in Paul's day did not think highly of humility. In fact we have no record of the use of this Greek word before Paul used it. People accepted it as natural that a person should make himself as great as he could in the sight of others. So it is today. The person who follows Christ has to go a different way. Read John 13:1-15. He cannot exalt his Saviour and exalt himself at the same time.

The second quality is *meekness*, the opposite of self-importance. It means submitting in obedience to God

and to His Word (see James 1:21). It means submitting
to other people (Paul will have more to say about this
in 5:21), and not trying to dominate or control them.
Numbers 12:3 says that 'Moses was very meek, more
than all men that were on the face of the earth'. From
the story of his life, we know how humble he was before
God, and before men too, even though he was their
appointed leader.

Thirdly there is *patience*. This word is used in the
New Testament for the endurance of suffering and
trial and difficulty (James 5:10), but especially for
patience with people. God has been patient with us in
spite of all our stubborn resistance to His ways (see
Romans 2:4). If we are walking worthily of our calling,
we must show that same patience with other people
(see 1 Corinthians 13:4).

Then fourthly comes *forbearance*. This means much
the same as 'long-suffering', but it especially concerns
our attitude to the person with whom we find it hard
to live, the person who annoys and provokes us, and
even tries to do us harm. If we are Christ's we will not
return evil for evil, but good for evil, and by the grace
of Christ we will love even when no love comes back in
return. See Matthew 5:38–48; 18:21–22.

b. Qualities of life in fellowship

The four qualities that Paul has named in verse 2
are necessary if, in our personal lives, we are to live
worthily of God's call. We need them also for the sake
of unity. Where there is pride, self-importance, self-
centredness and impatience, quarrels quickly come.
Then the unity that God has given us is broken, and
so our witness to Christ is spoilt. (See John 13:35;
17:21.) So with all our strength we are urged to keep
the unity of the Spirit in the bond of peace. The

apostle has more to say about this unity in the verses
that follow.

Prayer. *Lord God Almighty, Thou hast called us to live
in the world as Thy people and to bear witness to Thy name.
Help us to do so in humility and patience and love, striving to
avoid all bitterness, quarrelling and divisions, so that through
us the world may see Thy love, Thy peace, Thy power, and
Thy truth, in Jesus Christ our only Saviour.* AMEN.

Further Study. 1. What reasons does the Bible give
for Christians living in humility before God and before
their fellow men? See Exodus 20:25–26; Ecclesiastes
5:1–2; Isaiah 6:1–5; 66:1–2; Micah 6:8; Luke 18:9–14;
John 13:1–17; Philippians 2:1–8.

2. The Greek word used in verse 3 for 'eager' is
actually a verb and we find it also in 1 Thessalonians
2:17; 2 Timothy 2:15 and 2 Peter 1:10,15; 3:14. How
does the use of the word in these verses help us to
understand its meaning here?

Study 25. THE UNITY OF CHRISTIANS

**'There is one body and one Spirit, just as you
were called to the one hope that belongs to your
call, one Lord, one faith, one baptism, one God
and Father of us all, who is above all and through
all and in all'** (4:4–6).

We do not have to make unity and fellowship. We
have to guard it, and not allow it to be spoilt by jealousy
or strife. The unity is there. It is God's gift. When true
Christians meet – although they may be of different
race, of different ages, one may be rich and the other
poor, one educated and the other not – they should
immediately recognize that they are one. They have a

faith that is the same, they have a way of life that is the same, they are of the same family in Christ – and these things are greater than all the differences between them. Paul now gives seven foundations of that unity.

1. They are brought into *one body*. The repeated New Testament teaching is that the church is not just the collection of those who believe. It is the body of Christ. As we believe in Jesus Christ, we are not only joined to Him and receive personally the gift of eternal life – we are also made members of His body. We belong together just as the different parts of the human body belong together. Paul has more to say about this later. Here we must see that it means that we can never disregard our fellow Christians; we must not divide ourselves from them. God has brought us to be one body.

2. There is also *one Spirit*, one and the same Spirit of God who lives in all of us who belong to Him (see Romans 8:9–10). The same Spirit directs us all in the same ways – and so we have the 'fellowship of the Holy Spirit'. In our daily experience we all share the most wonderful blessing possible – God's Spirit in us. This blessing divides us off from those who do not know it, and binds us together in one with all who know it. (See also 1 Corinthians 12:13.)

3. We have *one hope that belongs to our calling*. We share the same call of God (verse 1), to know Him and serve Him now; and we have the same destiny awaiting us, to live for ever with the Lord. If we will be together then for eternity, how foolish it is to think of not wanting to worship and work and witness together for Him now!

4. We have *one Lord*. Jesus Christ is our Master to whom we owe all our loyalty. If we are fighting for Him, it is foolish and disloyal to strive one with another, or to refuse to join forces one with another to make His cause victorious in the world.

5. We have *one faith*. We depend on the same Lord, and draw all our strength from Him as we trust in Him. We have the same great beliefs – beliefs that should bind us together. Outside us is the vast non-Christian world of men who do not share these beliefs. We are one in the truth of the gospel, and with one voice should witness to those who do not know this good news in Christ.

6. All who come to Christ in faith are, by His command, baptized into Him. There is *one baptism*, the same for all who name the name of Christ. We may differ over detail in our understanding of the meaning of baptism; we may differ in the way that we baptize; but by baptism we are reckoned outwardly and visibly no longer with the non-Christian world, but with Christ and His people. We accept His grace and His calling, and determine that we will live for Him and 'fight manfully under His banner' to the end of our lives. No matter what our background or race or nation (see Galatians 3:27–28), we are baptized into one family (1 Corinthians 12:13).

7. Finally we have the *one God and Father of us all, who is above all and through all and in all*. This great God is our God. He has shown us His ways. He has given us His Son. He has come by His Spirit into our lives. We believe in Him as Lord and Creator, over all. We believe in Him as Preserver of all, Provider for all. We believe that He fills and controls His world. If such beliefs unite us, and the vast non-Christian world surrounds us, rejecting (but needing) this saving truth of God, should we find it hard to live with our fellow Christians, and want to separate ourselves from them?

Prayer. *Lord God, Thou hast graciously shown Thyself to us in Jesus Christ, and in Him made us one family, one body, one people. Help us seriously to lay to heart the great dangers we* *are in by our unhappy divisions in the church. May we so humbly learn of Thee that we may be led into the unity of Thy truth, and may we so humbly live together in love that no personal desires of ours may hinder fellowship and unity. So may the world see Thy glory in the lives of Thy people; and may many be led to Thee, through Jesus Christ our Lord.*

AMEN.

Further Study. 1. Consider with these verses other New Testament passages that speak of Christian unity, such as 1 Corinthians 10:16–17; 12:12–13 and Galatians 3:26–28.

2. Study 1 Corinthians 1:10–17 and 3:1–9, and consider how far the divisions among us in the church today arise from jealousies and a desire for personal power, and how much they come from genuine differences of conviction concerning the truth of Christ.

4:7–16. THE SPIRIT'S GIFTS TO THE CHURCH

THE LAST few verses have emphasized the unity of the church, but this unity is not uniformity. That is, the church is not made up of members who are intended to be all the same. It is said that no two flowers are ever exactly alike. It is certainly true that no two people in the world are just the same; and no two members of the church have exactly the same gifts. The unity of the church is like that of the body – all its members are different and have different work to do; and if the body is healthy, they all work together. The different gifts which the Spirit gives to us are what the apostle is speaking of in this section.

Study 26. THE VARIED GIFTS OF GOD

'But grace was given to each of us according to the measure of Christ's gift. Therefore it is said,

"When he ascended on high he led a host of captives,
and he gave gifts to men."

(In saying, "He ascended," what does it mean but that he had also descended into the lower parts of the earth? He who descended is he who also ascended far above all the heavens, that he might fill all things.) And his gifts were that some should be apostles, some prophets, some

evangelists, some pastors and teachers, for the equipment of the saints, for the work of ministry, for building up the body of Christ' (4:7–12).

a. Gifts for each one

The Spirit of God has left none of us without a gift. If we belong to God, He has a piece of work that we alone can do, and we have His gift to make it possible for us to do it. We should not ask whose gift is greater and whose is smaller. God in His wisdom and His grace has arranged that 'each of us' has the gift He intends us to have. In the early church there were apostles, prophets, evangelists, pastors, and teachers. 1 Corinthians 12:28 adds other gifts to the list, and not only those whom we call the 'ministers' of the church are included. Every member has received a gift (see 1 Corinthians 12:4–7).

b. Gifts of the ascended Lord

When we realize how great the Giver is, we should treasure the gift more, and want to use it rightly. He, our Lord Jesus Christ, came down to this world below. He humbled Himself and became Man, so that He might fill this world with the glory of His presence. He came down to save and redeem the world, and to claim it as His own. Then, having conquered the powers of evil, He rose triumphant, He ascended 'far above all the heavens'. That means that He has the place of highest authority. He is Lord of all. He has led His enemies captive. He is able to give to His people whatever He wishes. So He gives us His Spirit, and all the gifts and blessings of the Spirit. (See John 7:39; 14:12–14; Acts 2:33.) Through us now He wants His presence to be known in all the world, and all things to be made 'captive to obey Christ' (2 Corinthians 10:5).

c. The purpose of the gifts

There are other ways in which the apostle speaks of the purpose of these gifts of the Spirit that each one of us has received. Three things are mentioned in verse 12, and perhaps each depends on the one before it. First, the gifts of the Spirit are given 'for the equipment of the saints'. The word that Paul uses here for 'equipment' is used in Matthew 4:21 for the repairing of the disciples' nets, in Hebrews 11:3 for God's work in bringing the whole universe into the order that He intended it to have. So it means here that by the gifts of the Spirit, each Christian should be brought to live that good and healthy spiritual life that God intends for us. And that is not the end; we should be brought to that state of spiritual health for 'the work of ministry', that is, so that we can each serve our Lord and our fellows humbly and faithfully in all those good works that He has planned for us (see 2:10). The purpose of this, moreover, is the 'building up [of] the body of Christ'. The church is built up as it increases in numbers by people being won into it. It is also built up when it becomes strong in love (verse 16) and in truth (verse 15).

Prayer. *Lord Jesus, our risen and ascended Master, we thank Thee for the gifts of Thy Spirit which Thou hast poured out on each of us as members of Thy church. May we use what Thou hast given us, humbly serving our fellows, strengthening our fellow Christians, building up Thy body in love and truth and unity, to the glory of Thy wonderful name, now and for ever.* AMEN.

Notes. 1. In verse 8, Psalm 68:18 is being used. It spoke of the Lord returning in triumph after conquering the enemies of His people. It is applied here to

Christ's triumph by His death and resurrection. The Psalm spoke of the Conqueror receiving gifts; here the apostle thinks more of the gifts that He is able to give because of His triumph.

2. In verses 9–10 we do not need to think of 'places', of heaven high up and of earth down below. But this is the best way in which we can be helped to understand the glory and greatness of God, who has power and authority over all the universe, and of the way that Christ humbled Himself to enter into our life (see Philippians 2:6–9).

3. In the New Testament 'the twelve' stand out first and foremost as the 'apostles'; but Paul and Barnabas, James the Lord's brother, and Silas, are also called 'apostles'. When the word is used in the New Testament it is sometimes hard to be sure whether it means an 'apostle' or simply a 'messenger', but from 1 Corinthians 9:1–2 it seems that an 'apostle' was one who had seen the risen Lord and had been sent out by Him to do His work. The 'prophets' mentioned here and in 2:20 and 3:5 are not Old Testament prophets, but those who in the days of the early church were given inspired words to speak from God to the people. (See Acts 11:27–28; 15:32; 21:9,11; 1 Corinthians 14:24–32.) 'Evangelists' seem to have been men who, under the leadership of the apostles, travelled about doing preaching work. The 'pastors' and 'teachers' were those who, by their spiritual care and their instruction, built up the members of the church in their faith.

Further Study. 1. What teaching can we gain from these verses and from other New Testament passages (such as John 14:12–13; 16:7; Romans 8:34) about the meaning that the ascension of Jesus has for us?

2. Compare the teaching of verses 11–12 with that

of Galatians 6:1-2 and Hebrews 3:12-14 (and other similar passages) concerning the responsibility of Christians one for another.

Study 27. MATURITY AND UNITY

His gifts are to be used 'until we all attain to the unity of the faith and of the knowledge of the Son of God, to mature manhood, to the measure of the stature of the fullness of Christ; so that we may no longer be children, tossed to and fro and carried about with every wind of doctrine, by the cunning of men, by their craftiness in deceitful wiles. Rather, speaking the truth in love, we are to grow up in every way into him who is the head, into Christ, from whom the whole body, joined and knit together by every joint with which it is supplied, when each part is working properly, makes bodily growth and upbuilds itself in love' (4:13-16).

Verse 12 has said that the purpose of the gifts of the Spirit is the growth of the church, the body of Christ. Each individual Christian must grow from a babe, newborn in Christ, up through childhood, to adulthood. The whole church, itself like a human body with many members belonging together, must grow. There are some things that are the marks of childhood, and other things that are the marks of adult life, as Paul says in 1 Corinthians 13:11.

a. The marks of childhood

A young child is easily influenced, in the right way, or in the wrong way. Those who are young in the faith of Christ, and not yet strong in Him, are easily led. Where there is false teaching, they may be influenced by it without realizing it. There are those who try to deceive others; and the devil uses them to turn people aside from the ways of Christ. Paul describes in another way also those who are easily turned aside from the faith. They are like a little boat, tossed to and fro by the waves; whereas the Christian should be like a ship at anchor, its anchor holding firm whatever storms of temptation, of difficulty, or of false teaching there may be around it. (See Hebrews 6:18-20.)

b. The marks of adulthood

A firm hold of truth is one of the marks of a person who is an adult in Christ. He is not turned aside from the truth, in what he believes, in what he speaks, or in what he does. (The word that Paul uses in verse 15 means more than 'speaking the truth' – 'living in truth' is nearer to its meaning.) He also has grown 'in love'. Some people hold the truth, but without love in their hearts. The great commandment of Christ is love (John 13:34). We can only grow up in the Christian life as we grow in love.

c. Growth into unity

When we grow in love, we grow in unity. A family is united when there is strong love between its different members. The spokes of a wheel are nearest to one another when they are nearest to the centre. If we are really growing into Christ, as Paul says in verse 15, we must be growing in love, and we must be growing near together in the unity that God intends Christians to have. In all our thoughts about Christian unity, we must keep in mind two things, truth and love. These verses speak of them both. There is 'the unity of the faith', and this grows as we grow in the knowledge of the Son of God, and of His ways and His purposes. We cannot neglect truth when we strive for unity. But we must not neglect love either. Jesus Christ is described in John 1:14 as 'full of grace and truth'. As individual Christians, and as the body of Christ, we only grow towards 'the measure of the stature of the fullness of Christ' when we grow both in grace and truth.

d. The way of growth

These verses tell us also how growth from a babe in Christ to a man or woman of God is possible, and how the church itself grows. It is growth 'into Christ' (verse 15) and 'from' Him (verse 16). As we come to live more and more 'in Him', and as we receive from Him, so we grow. He is the Head, and we must be under His direction, obedient to Him. But growth in unity and maturity in the church, in another way, depends on us. There is that which every part of the body must *do* (verse 16). Each must use his or her spiritual gift (verse 7) for the building up of the whole (verse 12). Each member of the body must do its part for the body to be healthy and to grow and work as it should; but also each member must work rightly in relation to every other member. The thumb cannot do its work except in right relation with the rest of the hand. The foot cannot do its work except in connection with the leg, and the arm, and the brain that controls it. The church can grow only as its members work together, each realizing the gifts and the work given to others. And the growth of the church that the Lord of the church wants is (as we have seen) growth 'in love' (verse 16). When the church grows in love, love for its Lord and love for others, it will surely also grow in numbers. There is no real witness, and very little winning of others, except by love.

Prayer. *Almighty Father, help us to 'grow in the grace and knowledge of our Lord and Saviour Jesus Christ. To him be the glory both now and to the day of eternity. Amen.'*
(2 Peter 3:18.)

Further Study. 1. Study carefully the words used in these verses for growth into maturity, and compare the teaching of 1 Corinthians 3:1–3; 14:20 and Hebrews 5:11–14.
2. Study 1 Corinthians 12:12–31 as a detailed explanation of verse 16.

4:17-24. THE NEW NATURE OF THE CHRISTIAN

THE LAST few verses have given us a picture of the growth of the Christian and the growth of the church in Christ. But such spiritual growth is possible only when the old godless way of life is rejected. That life led step by step in a certain direction – away from God, away from the truth. The Christian must walk in that direction no longer; he has turned to walk towards God. Previously his life was guided by selfish desires. This way of life is to be put off as a person puts off old, ragged clothes, throws them away, and never takes them up again. The new life he is to put on like a new, clean set of clothes.

Study 28.
THE OLD WAY TO BE REJECTED

'Now this I affirm and testify in the Lord, that you must no longer live as the Gentiles do, in the futility of their minds; they are darkened in their understanding, alienated from the life of God because of the ignorance that is in them, due to their hardness of heart; they have become callous and have given themselves up to licentiousness, greedy to practise every kind of uncleanness. You did not so learn Christ! – assuming that you have heard about him and were taught in him, as the truth is in Jesus. Put off

your old nature which belongs to your former manner of life and is corrupt through deceitful lusts' (4:17–22).

What the apostle says here, he wants to say with great emphasis (verse 17). He is sure that he is speaking 'in the Lord', and telling the Lord's will for all who name the name of Christ. There are some key words in these verses:

Futility. 'Futility' or 'vanity' is the key thought of the book of Ecclesiastes in the Old Testament, as it describes the life that has not found its purpose in God. Without Christ life is empty, and purposeless. Apart from the desire to know and do God's wonderful will, everything is vain and profitless. If we are 'in Christ' that is so *no longer*. We are set free from aimless living (see 1 Peter 1:18). We are given purpose and direction, and must never again go back to the vain, godless life.

Darkness. When we did not know God we were in the dark. We did not see the truth or understand it. Now we have been called 'out of darkness into his marvellous light' (1 Peter 2:9). We are in darkness *no longer*, and we must never turn from the light that we know, or we will surely stumble and fall, like those who try to walk about in the night without a lamp.

Alienation. One nation can be on friendly terms with another, or the two may be alienated. This Epistle has already shown us very clearly that by our sin we were alienated from God (2:1–3) and from the life that He intended us to have. But when we receive the mercy and forgiveness of Christ (2:4–8), we are alienated *no longer*. Never must we go back to the ways that make us rebellious subjects, with hearts hardened against His loving will. We are His children (1:5), and the Lord Jesus Christ says also to us, 'You are my friends if you do what I command you' (John 15:14).

Uncleanness. When the light of God has been shut out, and everything seems vain and empty, then there is no feeling for what is beautiful, good and true. A person does what he wants to do. God's law is rejected. Uncleanness of word and action, and impurity of sexual relationships often result. 'Greediness' describes the kind of life that follows. A person says, 'I will have what I want, and I do not care what anyone else thinks.' The old godless life led in that direction. But for the Christian the direction is changed – *no longer* can there be uncleanness and greediness. The door has been shut on them for ever.

About all these things the apostle says, 'you did not so learn Christ.' You have come to Him. You have heard His voice. You have been taught by Him. You live in Him. So the old nature – lifeless, valueless, deceitful as it is – must be put away. It must be treated as dead, and knocked back every time that it tries to lift its head (Romans 6:11). No longer evil but good; no longer darkness but light; no longer enemies but friends of God; no longer I but Christ; this is the Christian's rule.

Prayer. *Gracious heavenly Father, Thou hast called us in Thy grace from living without purpose, without peace and without any true joy, and brought us to find true life in Christ. By Thy mighty power may we never again go back to the things that grieve Thee, but daily and in every part of life seek and do Thy will, in Jesus Christ our Saviour.* AMEN.

Notes. 1. Verse 17 means that spiritually they were Gentiles before, separated by sin from the chosen people of God. Now they are so no longer (compare 1 Corinthians 12:2). They now are the people of God, members of God's Israel (see 2:11–21 and Galatians 6:16).

2. The word used at the beginning of verse 19 referred originally to the absence of feelings of pain and sorrow; here it is used to mean that such people had no more sense of the truth of God, nor did they feel in their conscience any shame because of sin.

Further Study. 1. Study in other parts of the New Testament the word used for 'greedy' in verse 19. You will find it (sometimes translated 'covetous') in 5:3,5; in Luke 12:15; Colossians 3:5; and the corresponding verb is in 1 Thessalonians 4:6. See the way that it is applied to selfish desire for material things or to selfish sexual desire (note how the two stand together in Hebrews 13:4-6).

2. Verse 22 speaks of our desires as deceitful. Consider other places in the Bible where sin is regarded as deceitful, promising joy and gain that it cannot really give. For example, see Genesis 3; Deuteronomy 11:16; Matthew 13:22; Romans 7:11 and Hebrews 3:13.

Study 29. THE NEW NATURE

'. . . And be renewed in the spirit of your minds, and put on the new nature, created after the likeness of God in true righteousness and holiness' (4:23-24).

The last six verses have spoken of the way that the old nature, the selfish, sinful way of living, is to be set aside, as a person throws away his old, worn-out clothes. A new nature is to be put on – like new clothes, though of course it is not just something outward, but something that changes the whole life of the person. There are three ways in which the apostle expresses this.

95

a. A new mind

In verse 17 Paul has spoken of the 'futility' of the minds of those who are far from God. When we come back to God through Jesus Christ, we have new thoughts; we come to think in a new way. Our minds are renewed. Instead of putting self first, and thinking of our own gain, we put God first, and we choose His will. This is a complete change in our way of thinking; the apostle speaks of it in Romans 12:2 as 'the renewal' of the 'mind', to 'prove what is the will of God, what is good and acceptable and perfect'.

b. A new person

God made us as His children, 'in his own image' in the beginning. But through sin this nature that we were given was spoiled. God wants to do nothing less for us than to make us new in Jesus Christ. His work, as we have already seen in 2:10,15, is nothing less than a new creation (see also 2 Corinthians 5:17). Paul speaks of this creation as 'after the likeness of God'; Colossians 3:10 says you 'have put on the new nature, which is being renewed in knowledge after the image of its creator'.

c. A new character

If we are created again by God, so as to be brought back to His 'image' in which we were made in the beginning, then we must live as new people. We must have a new character. 'Righteousness' and 'holiness' are the two words that describe this. Righteousness means doing always what is right and true towards our fellow men. Holiness means doing what is pure and good before God. If we obey those two laws that sum

96

up all the commandments (Matthew 22:36–40), then we will express the new character that the Christian ought to express. There is no other way. There is no lower standard. We are new men and women, and we must treat the old nature as put away for ever.

Prayer. *Lord, by Thy grace and forgiveness the many sins of our old way of life are taken away. Help us to live out the new life that Thou hast created in us. In our thoughts, and so in our words and actions, may there be only those things that are right and loving and true. So may we be made more like Thy Son, our Saviour Jesus Christ.* AMEN.

Note. There are two words in the Greek New Testament for 'new'; the first means 'new' as distinct from 'old' (like food that is not stale) – this word is used in verse 24; the second means 'new' in the sense of 'young' (like a 'new' baby) – this word is used in the verb in verse 23. This verb is also in the present continuous tense, showing that it is God's purpose for our lives to be constantly being made fresh and new, young and strong, by His Holy Spirit.

Further Study. 1. Study other places in the New Testament which speak of putting off the old nature and putting on the new – for example see Romans 13:12; Colossians 3:9–10; Hebrews 12:1; James 1:21; 1 Peter 2:1.

2. Study further the words 'righteousness' and 'holiness', where they are found together (as in Luke 1:75; 1 Thessalonians 2:10 and Titus 1:8), and where they are found by themselves.

4:25 – 5:2. THE NEW CONDUCT OF THE CHRISTIAN

THE APOSTLE has been speaking of the things which must be put away from the Christian life (verse 22), and the things which must be put on (verse 24). He says more in this section – especially about putting away all that is untrue and unloving, and putting on truth and honesty, love and kindness.

Study 30.
TRUTH IN WORD AND ACTION

'Therefore, putting away falsehood, let every one speak the truth with his neighbour, for we are members one of another. Be angry but do not sin; do not let the sun go down on your anger, and give no opportunity to the devil. Let the thief no longer steal, but rather let him labour, doing honest work with his hands, so that he may be able to give to those in need. Let no evil talk come out of your mouths, but only such as is good for edifying, as fits the occasion, that it may impart grace to those who hear. And do not grieve the Holy Spirit of God, in whom you were sealed for the day of redemption' (4:25–30).

Paul gives four particular exhortations in these verses, and to each one he adds an important reason.

a. Truth to replace falsehood

There is no place for lying in the Christian's life.
(Paul is quoting Zechariah 8:16 in what he says in
verse 25.) He is to be a man of his word, always and
under all circumstances. His 'Yes' is to mean 'Yes' and
his 'No' to mean 'No' (Matthew 5:37). He is not to
deceive others, about himself, or about anything else.
He must be someone who can be trusted. Then notice
the reason that the apostle gives. 'We are members
one of another.' We belong together, especially in the
family of the Christian church, as members of one body.
We should be able to trust one another. The old Greek
writer Chrysostom said, 'If the eye sees a snake, does it
deceive the foot? if the tongue tastes what is bitter,
does it deceive the stomach?' So in the Christian's life
there must be no trying to deceive others, but truth and
trustworthiness in everything.

b. Right and wrong anger

Quoting the Old Testament again (Psalm 4:4), Paul
says, 'Be angry but do not sin.' It is not always wrong to
be angry. Our Lord Himself was angry – with those
who misused the Temple, and prevented it being used
as a house of prayer (see John 2:13–17); and with the
self-righteous, narrow-minded Pharisees, who did not
want Him to heal on the sabbath day (see Mark 3:1–6).
That was righteous anger. But anger is wrong when it
makes us bitter against people, and leads us to hate them
and to want to do or say evil against them. So Paul
wisely says, 'do not let the sun go down on your anger.'
If you have been angry for a good cause, do not keep
your strong feelings. The reason for this is that it can
so easily provide an open door for the devil. We feel
angry against a person. Perhaps at first we are right to

be angry; but then we let anger grow, and it becomes hatred. Fellowship is broken, and we no longer walk in the light and in love one with the other. This is the work that the devil is always trying to do. We must resist him (see James 4:7 and 1 Peter 5:8–9), and give him no chance to do his evil work.

c. Honest work instead of dishonesty

Whatever there may have been in a person's life before he became a Christian, when he comes to belong to Christ there is to be no more dishonesty. Stealing means more than robbing the house or the possessions of another person. If we refuse to pay our lawful tax, if we do not give a good day's work for the day's wages that we get, if we are dishonest in business, that is stealing. Everything of that kind must be a thing of the past. Good work, faithfully done, must be the mark of the Christian's life. Then he will truly earn his money. And what is the reason for this? Not only that he may have wages, honestly gained, to use for himself – but that he will have something to give to those in need. Personal gain should never be the aim of the Christian's life – rather he should aim to be as useful and as helpful to others as he can.

d. Words of grace instead of bad language

The world is full of bad language. Paul uses a word here that means 'rotten', and is used for 'rotten' fruit. Bad fruit soon makes the good fruit next to it bad as well. Bad language can work like that, too – leading others to bad thoughts, bad words and bad deeds. The Christian's words can be used for good, just as his money can. They can 'impart grace', as the words of Christ did (Luke 4:22). They can help the discouraged, the disappointed, the sad. They can turn others to Christ, to find in Him all that they need. It is good for the Christian to think what the need may be in some-one else's life, and speak a word that will help and uplift.

There is a reason for this exhortation too. We have been given the Spirit of God, and He wants to keep us safe till the day of our final redemption (see 1:13–14 and notes). The Spirit of God is the Holy Spirit, and we grieve Him whenever we allow anything unholy into our lives. He is also the Spirit who wants to guide and inspire our words; we grieve Him when we refuse to let Him bring words of truth and love and grace to our lips.

Prayer. *Lord of all grace and goodness, help us to resist the devil and to let Thy Spirit strengthen us to think and say and do only those things which are true, honourable, just, pure, lovely and of good report, that we may live as Christ's men and women in the world, for His name's sake.* AMEN.

Notes. 1. In verse 26 Paul is quoting the Greek version of Psalm 4:4 which is a little different from the Hebrew which our Bible translates, but both give a good meaning.

2. The word used for 'labour' in verse 28 means the hard work that makes a person tired, indicating that the Christian is never to try to avoid working as hard as he can. See 1 Thessalonians 4:11 and 2 Thessalonians 3:10–12.

Further Study. 1. In connection with verse 28 see what an important place giving to the poor has in the New Testament, even in the cases of our Lord and His disciples, who had very little to give. See Matthew 19:21; Luke 14:13; John 13:29; Acts 2:44–45; 4:32–37;

6:1–4; Romans 15:26–27; 1 Corinthians 16:1–3; 2 Corinthians 8 and 9 and Galatians 2:10.

2. Study with these verses other New Testament passages that speak of the Christian's speech, such as Colossians 3:16; 4:6 and James 3.

Study 31. LOVE, LIKE GOD'S OWN LOVE

'Let all bitterness and wrath and anger and clamour and slander be put away from you, with all malice, and be kind to one another, tender-hearted, forgiving one another, as God in Christ forgave you.

Therefore be imitators of God, as beloved children. And walk in love, as Christ loved us and gave himself up for us, a fragrant offering and sacrifice to God' (4:31–5:2).

There are still more things to be put away, and one supremely important thing to be put on in the Christian life. Love is to be put on, and everything that is against love must be put away. For love is the clearest mark of the Christian life (see John 13:35; 1 Corinthians 13; Galatians 5:22; and 1 John 2:7–11; 3:10–18,23; 4:7–21). And Christian love has no lower standard than the love of God that we know in Jesus Christ.

a. Love shown in kindness

In verse 31 six things are named, which the Christian is not to allow in his life. First, 'bitterness' – the poisonous thoughts of hatred for others. Secondly, 'wrath' – the feelings of anger that rise up in us when someone says or does something against us personally. Then there is that settled kind of 'anger' against which

Paul has already spoken in verse 26, the anger that we let
go on day after day. 'Clamour' means the angry and loud
shouting against others, when we want everyone to
hear the wrong that we feel that someone else has done.
'Slander' includes every kind of false or evil speaking
against men, and against God as well. Lastly, there
is 'malice', the feelings in our hearts that lead us to
want to harm some other person. All of these must go
out, and be replaced by love, love that shows itself in
kindness and tenderness. And kindness cannot stop
with thoughts; it must express itself in words and actions,
as God's kindness has expressed itself to us (see 2:7).

b. Love shown in forgiveness

The things of which Paul has spoken in verse 31
often come because we feel that someone else has
wronged us. We may be right, and the other person
wrong. We are still to love, and to forgive, because only
a spirit of forgiveness can put away bitterness, anger
and malice. We must forgive, because God has forgiven
us; and we must forgive as completely as God forgives
us (see Psalm 103:12). Our Lord teaches us to pray
'forgive us our trespasses', but only 'as we forgive them
that trespass against us'; and after He gave that prayer
He spoke solemn words when He said, 'If you do not
forgive men their trespasses, neither will your Father
forgive your trespasses' (Matthew 6:15). He gave the
same lesson as solemnly in the parable of the ungrateful
debtor in Matthew 18:21–35.

c. Love shown in self-sacrifice

'Imitators of God' – this is a high standard. It would
be impossibly high, if He had not promised His Spirit of
love to dwell in our hearts. We are children of God –

this is our privilege, as we have faith in Jesus Christ (see John 1:12). It is also our responsibility to be like Him. Above all, we are to be like Him in love, and we are to walk step by step along the road of life in love. The love of God showed itself supremely in that He gave Himself for us (see John 10:11,17 and Galatians 2:20). Our love is only like His when we give ourselves, even to the point of sacrifice, for others (see 1 John 3:16). When a woman, who loved our Lord deeply, poured her costly ointment over the feet of Jesus, we read that the house was filled with the fragrance (John 12:3). So when our love expresses itself in self-giving, in self-sacrifice, there will be a loveliness and a fragrance that will be a blessing to many (see 2 Corinthians 2:14–16 and Philippians 4:18).

Prayer. *Lord, Thou knowest that thoughts of hatred and bitterness, of evil and resentment, often come into our hearts. By Thy Spirit pour Thy love into our hearts, that everything that is unloving and unforgiving may go out; so may we walk daily in love, through and for the sake of Jesus Christ who loved us and gave Himself for us.* AMEN.

Further Study. 1. Consider other New Testament passages which emphasize the Christian's duty to be like God, or like Christ, and which indicate the way in which this is possible, *e.g.* see Matthew 5:7, 44, 45, 48; Luke 6:36; Philippians 2:15; 1 Peter 1:14–17; Galatians 4:6–7.

2. Study further the meaning of Christ's death being spoken of as a 'sacrifice' – *e.g.* see Matthew 26:28; John 1:29; 1 Corinthians 5:7; Hebrews 7:27; 9:14; 10:10–14.

5:3-14. LIGHT IN PLACE OF DARKNESS

HERE THE thought of the things to be 'put on' and 'put off' continues. In this section it is all those things that, morally and spiritually, are of darkness that must be put away. Christians are children of light, and must show this in all that they do.

Study 32. PURITY OF LIFE

'But immorality and all impurity or covetousness must not even be named among you, as is fitting among saints. Let there be no filthiness, nor silly talk, nor levity, which are not fitting; but instead let there be thanksgiving. Be sure of this, that no immoral or impure man, or one who is covetous (that is, an idolater), has any inheritance in the kingdom of Christ and of God. Let no one deceive you with empty words, for it is because of these things that the wrath of God comes upon the sons of disobedience' (5:3-6).

These verses deal chiefly with sins connected with sex. Sex is one of the most beautiful of God's gifts to man. Marriage should express the deepest human love of man and woman. In love, one man and one woman, made to complement one another, live in life-long partnership. From their love come the gift of children, and the blessing of the security and joy of the home. When sex is perverted, all these gifts are spoilt. Paul does not mean that sexual sins are the worst of all sins, but he does mean to show us how serious they are, when he says that 'it is because of these things that the wrath of God comes upon the sons of disobedience'.

They are among the most obvious signs of evil in the lives of those who live without respect for the law of God. Sexual sins are serious in the sight of God, because through them marriage is spoilt, and homes are broken up. Where there are sexual relationships outside of marriage, children may be brought into the world without the loving care of parents and the security of a home. God's judgment rests on these sins, the apostle says, but he does not mean that they are unforgivable sins. 1 Corinthians 6:9-11 shows how those who have been guilty of these sins can, by repentance and faith, find forgiveness and cleansing. But no-one can continue in these sins or any other sins, unrepentant, and at the same time enter the kingdom of God. They are sins that must be put away, and they are not to be talked about in a way which would tempt others to do them.

Again Paul speaks of the way that the Christian must act – to 'put away' and to 'put on', to hate all that is impure, and to love the pure and lovely.

a. Hating the evil and impure

Paul describes sexual immorality in two ways. First, it is against purity of living. It is uncleanness. It contradicts and rejects the purpose of God for manhood and womanhood – one man and one woman joining in the loving and life-long union of marriage, and having children whom they bring up in the security of the home they create. Secondly, sexual immorality is greed or covetousness; it is seeking what does not belong to us. Such uncleanness and such greed we must put away from our thoughts, and so from our lives. Our conversation is to be kept pure also. The world seems to love the stories that speak of sexual perversion, and that provoke unlawful passion. Paul probably has these chiefly in mind when he speaks of 'silly talk' and 'levity'. There is no place in the Christian's conversation for anything which deals lightly with sin, or leads others into temptation, or makes one ashamed. The apostle intends no rebuke for good, clean humour and fun; the danger lies in that sort of wittiness which leads a person away from what is pure and lovely into sin.

b. Seeking the pure and the good

The thought-life of the Christian is to be filled with the beautiful and the true and the good, as Paul says in Philippians 4:8. Here he speaks especially of the Christian's words. In the place of 'filthiness', 'silly talk' and 'levity', there is to be 'thanksgiving'. And the word he uses is connected with the word 'grace' which he used in 4:29 when dealing with the Christian's conversation. 'Thanksgiving' is a rule of life for the Christian. If you think of sex and speak of it, then dwell on its beauty and loveliness, in the spirit of thankfulness for God's wonderful gift. If you think of other people and speak of them, try to speak about the things in their lives for which you can thank God. When there is thanksgiving and praise in our hearts and on our lips, sin will not easily enter there. 'Everything created by God is good, and nothing is to be rejected if it is received with thanksgiving' (1 Timothy 4:4). Here is a good test. Can you receive and use this gift, can you do what you have in mind to do, in a spirit of thanksgiving and praise to God?

Prayer. *Almighty God, the Giver of everything that is good and perfect, cleanse the thoughts of our hearts, and keep us* *pure, in thought, word and deed, hating everything that is contrary to Thy will, and living to Thy praise and glory in all our life and in all our relationships, through Jesus Christ our Saviour.* AMEN.

Notes. 1. In 4:19, as in verse 3 here, sexual uncleanness is connected with covetousness.

2. Covetousness, the greed for what is not rightly one's own, is idolatry (compare Colossians 3:5), because it is putting something as an idol or an object of one's desires before God and God's will.

Further Study. What other teaching does the New Testament give concerning the attitude that prevents a person inheriting the kingdom of God? See Matthew 5:20; John 3:5; 1 Corinthians 6:9; Galatians 5:21.

Study 33. CHILDREN OF LIGHT

'**Therefore do not associate with them, for once you were darkness, but now you are light in the Lord; walk as children of light (for the fruit of light is found in all that is good and right and true), and try to learn what is pleasing to the Lord. Take no part in the unfruitful works of darkness, but instead expose them. For it is a shame even to speak of the things that they do in secret; but when anything is exposed by the light it becomes visible, for anything that becomes visible is light. Therefore it is said,**
 "**Awake, O sleeper, and arise from the dead, and Christ shall give you light**" ' (5:7-14).

a. The change from darkness to light

The change from the old life, with its evil and

impurity, to the new life in Christ is like the change from darkness to light. You cannot have light and darkness at the same time. You may shut the doors of a room, cover its windows and every possible opening for the light, and you will have darkness. Open the doors and windows, and light will come in; you cannot then keep the darkness. Everything will be light. Apart from Christ we are in the dark, and the darkness of sin is in us – once we 'were darkness'. When we let Christ shine on us (verse 14), and come into our lives, a new day has dawned (Matthew 4:16; compare Luke 1:78–79). We are in the light, and the light is in us. As our life is 'in the Lord', we now 'are light' in Him. Jesus said 'I am the light of the world; he who follows me will not walk in the darkness, but will have the light of life' (John 8:12). He also said to those who, as His disciples, had let His light into their lives, 'You are the light of the world' (Matthew 5:14).

b. Walking in the light

If we have come to the Light of the world, darkness has gone from our lives. We are in the light. We are alight ourselves. The light must shine from us to others. This means that we must walk – we must take each step in our daily lives – as 'children of light'. A plant grows towards the light. It cannot grow strong without light, just as it cannot grow strong without air and water and good soil. By living in the light, it grows to its full size and bears fruit. There must be fruit in the lives of those who are 'children of light'. Only the things that are right will be seen in their lives, and nothing unclean or evil. Only the things that are true, and nothing that is dishonest in word or in action; only the things that are good will be there. Every opportunity of doing and saying what is good and kind will be taken. Every opportunity of showing the love and goodness of Christ will be used. There will then be no place left for 'the unfruitful works of darkness', the things that people are ashamed to do in the light. (Compare Romans 6:21 and Galatians 5:19–22.) What will matter most to us will be to find out and do 'what is pleasing unto the Lord'.

c. The effect of light on the darkness

We are 'light in the Lord'. We are called to live 'as children of light'. What then will be the effect of lives of light in the darkness of the world? They will make other people decide for the light or for the darkness. Some creatures love the darkness of night, like the owl and the bat. Others love the day. At night-time the moth comes to the light, though it burns itself in doing so. The cockroach, and other insects, try to run away from the light into whatever dark corner they can find. All men are either like the moth or like the cockroach. The light of Jesus Christ shines in the world. People may try to escape from His light into the darkness of their own self-chosen ways, where they will stumble and fall. Or they may come to the light. If we come to the light of Christ, His light will show up our deeds for what they are, just as the sunshine shows up a dusty room. We will have to confess the sinfulness of what we have done; but when we do this, He takes away the darkness of evil. There is then light in us; we are 'exposed' by Him (verse 13), and we become light.

Verse 14 gives us three very vivid pictures of the truth. Sin is sleep; to forsake sin is to wake up, to work and to enjoy the fullness of God's gifts. Sin is death; to forsake sin is to find life, eternal life with God (see 2:1–6). Sin is darkness; to forsake sin is to reject the darkness and let the light of Christ shine in on us.

Prayer. *O God, who art perfect light and in whom there is no darkness at all, may we be willing to let Thy light shine into the dark places of our lives. Show up our evil for what it truly is, and then take it away, and change us into light. So may our lives be the lives of the children of light, and bring light to those who are still in darkness; through Jesus Christ our Saviour.* AMEN.

Notes. 1. Some old copies of this Epistle had 'the fruit of the Spirit' in verse 9; but most likely the original reading was 'the fruit of the light'.

2. Verse 14 is not actually a quotation from the Old Testament, although some Old Testament passages have the thoughts that are in this verse (*e.g.* Isaiah 9:2; 26:19; 52:1; 60:1). Probably it is part of an old Christian hymn.

Further Study. 1. Along with the teaching about darkness and light in these verses, study John 3:19–21; 9:39–41 and 1 John 1:5–10.

2. Compare with verse 14 what is said about sleeping and waking in Mark 13:33–37; Romans 13:11–12 and 1 Thessalonians 5:4–8.

5:15-21. THE WAY OF WISDOM

BY A NUMBER of different illustrations the apostle has spoken of the two ways of life. The Christian is one who has put away the old and put on the new. He has put away dishonesty and bitterness and evil speaking, and put on truth and love and kindness. He has forsaken darkness, and become light. In this section Paul speaks about him living as one who is wise and not foolish.

Study 34. WISDOM INSTEAD OF FOLLY

'Look carefully then how you walk, not as unwise men but as wise, making the most of the time, because the days are evil. Therefore do not be foolish, but understand what the will of the Lord is' (5:15-17).

Here are three ways in which the Christian should be wise.

a. In principles of life

Yet again Paul uses the word 'walk'. He has spoken of taking one step after another through life 'in love' (verse 2), and 'as children of light' (verse 8). Now he speaks of walking 'not as unwise men but as wise'. God has given us 'wisdom and insight' (1:9); He has 'enlightened' our eyes (1:18). So we know His purpose for our lives. We know the way that He wants us to live. But in a world in which evil so often prevails over good,

and where the majority follow their own wisdom
rather than the wisdom of God, the Christian must
'look carefully'. He must keep a close watch on the
principles by which he guides his life, and see that they
are the wise principles that God has given, and not the
unwise ones suggested by the world or by his own
selfishness.

b. In use of time

A man shows wisdom – or folly – in the use of his
time, more than in almost any other way. Time does
not just flow on day by day, so that you can say, 'what
I don't do today, I can do tomorrow.' Each day has
its opportunities, opportunities that may not come
again. Those who are wise will buy up the opportunities
and use them to the full. 'So teach us to number our
days', the psalmist prayed, 'that we may get a heart of
wisdom' (Psalm 90:12). The time is short (1 Corinthians
7:29). None of us knows how long he has (see Luke
12:20-21 and James 4:13-17). 'The days are evil.'
We must not allow our days to get into the control of
the evil one. We should ask at the end of the day, 'What
work of abiding and eternal worth have I done today?'

c. In knowing God's will

We cannot be wise in using our time and opportunities, unless we know what God's will is for us. Verse 10
has spoken of the importance of being sure of 'what is
pleasing to the Lord'. God not only seeks to give us
wisdom concerning the great issues and purposes of
life. He intends us to seek and to know and to do His
will in the details of each day. The apostle gives a
command, 'do not be foolish, but understand what the
will of the Lord is'. If we do not understand the will of

the Lord, then we are foolish, because He has promised
to guide us, and He will surely keep His promise, if we
turn to Him. He will guide us in the great decisions
concerning our life-work, concerning marriage or any
other great issue, and in the little decisions about what
we should do each day and how we should use our time.
He wants to lead us to understand and to fulfil His will.
Romans 12:1–2 gives three conditions for this: (a) that
we give ourselves fully to God; (b) that we do not want
simply to be like the world; (c) that we let God renew
our minds, and work in our minds. Then we can 'prove
what is the will of God, what is good and acceptable
and perfect'.

Prayer. *Lord of all grace, we thank Thee that Thou hast
not left us to walk in darkness, but hast promised Thy light and
guidance for all our ways. So help us to know Thy will in
things great and small, in the use of our time, in the principles
of our lives, and in the details of each day. So may we not
waste the gifts and opportunities that Thou hast given us to
use to Thy glory.* AMEN.

Further Study. Consider with these verses the pro-
mises of God's guidance in such passages as Psalm 25:9;
22:8; 48:14; Isaiah 58:11; Luke 11:13; John 8:12;
16:13 and James 1:5–8; and considering these passages
in their context, what conditions do they give for
receiving God's guidance?

Study 35. THE FULLNESS OF THE SPIRIT

**'And do not get drunk with wine, for that is debau-
chery; but be filled with the Spirit, addressing
one another in psalms and hymns and spiritual
songs, singing and making melody to the Lord
with all your heart, always and for everything**

giving thanks in the name of our Lord Jesus Christ to God the Father.
Be subject to one another out of reverence for Christ' (5:18–21).

In the last few verses we have read the call to act wisely and not unwisely, using time and opportunities to the full. This leads the apostle to speak a few words against drunkenness. Drunkenness is foolish and wrong for the Christian for three reasons. (1) It is wasteful, causing the waste of God's gifts, and the waste of money. (2) It leads to 'debauchery' – that is, it leads people to act in a way that they cannot control; and how much harm has been done in the home, among friends, and in accidents, through drunkenness! (3) People drink so that they may get into a spirit of joy and merriment. They want to drown their sorrows, or find freedom from their fears or from their limitations. The Christian knows a better way to find joy and freedom, a better way to deal with sorrows or difficulties or disappointments. It is the way that he chooses when he allows the Spirit of God to possess, control and uplift him. (See the contrast between drunkenness and being filled with the Spirit in Acts 2:14–18 also.)

'Be filled with the Spirit'

This is a command, and it is addressed to every Christian. We are to let every part of our lives be possessed by Him, so that He is able to control all. It was the great promise of Christ Himself that He would give His Spirit to those who believe and are willing to receive Him (see John 14:16–18; 16:13). This promise came true on the day of Pentecost (Acts 2). It is still true. The promise is to us. The condition is that we should be willing to let Him come into every part of life, to inspire and to control.

115

The effect of being filled with the Spirit

In verses 19–21 Paul speaks of the results that will
follow if the Holy Spirit does fill our lives.

1 *Praise and thanksgiving.* If He lives fully in us, then
our lives will be full of praise. Praise expresses itself
in singing. At every time when there has been a great
movement of the Spirit in the life of the church,
Christians' lives have been full of singing. In the early
days of the church they sang psalms, and they made up
their own hymns. (Little parts of these we can probably
see in 4:4–6; 5:14; 1 Timothy 1:17; 2:5–6; 6:15–16;
2 Timothy 2:11–13; Revelation 4:11; 5:13 and 7:12.)
The great Reformers in the sixteenth century gave us
some of our greatest hymns. Later, hymns poured forth
from the leaders of the Evangelical Revival, John and
Charles Wesley, John Newton and many others. More
recently the Revival in East Africa has expressed itself
especially in the joy of singing. The individual Christian,
filled with the Spirit, will want to sing God's praises.
Paul and Silas could sing even in prison (Acts 16:25),
and could rejoice even in sufferings (see 2 Corinthians
11:18–33). If the Spirit fills our lives we will be able
'always' to be 'giving thanks', because in everything
we will find the blessing of His guidance, His supply of
all our need, and His strength in our witness to Jesus
Christ (Acts 1:8).

2. *Humble service.* The filling of the Spirit of God
does not, however, make the individual Christian free
to do as he pleases, without thinking of others. The
Spirit also leads us to 'reverence' Christ (that is, to
honour and obey Him), and to submit ourselves one to
another. In 2 Timothy 1:7 we read about the Holy
Spirit as the Spirit 'of power and love and self-control'.
He gives power and love, and also makes our lives
disciplined. We have seen that He is the Spirit who

gives fellowship in the church (see notes on 4:2–3). So if the Spirit is filling our lives, we will not want to lift up ourselves above others, but to serve others. We will not want to argue and quarrel, but, when it is not a matter of principle, we will let others have their way. The Spirit in us is the Spirit of Jesus; and Jesus, without doing any sin Himself, submitted Himself to wicked men, even to the cross.

Prayer. *Lord, fill my life in every part with Thy Spirit of love and power and discipline, and may His presence in my life be seen in joy and thanksgiving and humble service, for the sake of Jesus Christ.* AMEN.

Further Study. 1. What do such passages as Acts 2:1–4; 4:31 and 13:52 show were the results of people being filled with the Spirit?

2. How do the New Testament Epistles show the difficulties that arise when Christians do not submit themselves to one another in the work and the worship of the church? (*E.g.* see 1 Corinthians 1:10–17; 3:1–9; 14:26–33; Philippians 2:1–4 and 4:2.)

5:22 – 6:9. THE NEW RELATION-SHIPS OF THE CHRISTIAN

THE LAST section closed with a reminder of the duty of the Christian to submit to others, to be willing to serve, and not to be wanting all the time to press for his own rights or for his own way. This now has a special application to relationships in the Christian home – relationships between husbands and wives, children and parents, servants and masters.

Study 36.
LESSONS FOR WIVES AND HUSBANDS

'Wives, be subject to your husbands, as to the Lord. For the husband is the head of the wife as Christ is the head of the church, his body, and is himself its Saviour. As the church is subject to Christ, so let wives also be subject in everything to their husbands. Husbands, love your wives, as Christ loved the church and gave himself up for her, that he might sanctify her, having cleansed her by the washing of water with the word, that he might present the church to himself in splendour, without spot or wrinkle or any such thing, that she might be holy and without blemish. Even so husbands should love their wives as their own bodies. He who loves his wife loves himself. For no man ever hates his own flesh, but nourishes and cherishes it, as Christ does the

church, because we are members of his body. "For this reason a man shall leave his father and mother and be joined to his wife, and the two shall become one." This is a great mystery, and I take it to mean Christ and the church; however, let each one of you love his wife as himself, and let the wife see that she respects her husband' (5:22–33).

These verses speak of the duties of wives and husbands in the Christian home. It is impossible to tell fully what Christianity has done for womanhood. The Jewish man thanked God that he was not made a woman. In many societies there is far greater joy over the birth of a son than a daughter. Marriage customs in many places are such that a wife is treated as a possession rather than as a partner. Our Lord Himself showed equal care and concern for women as for men. Paul shows that men and women have equal right to all the spiritual blessings of Christ (Galatians 3:28). The Bible teaches that in marriage there is the union of two partners in love, so that they become one. Sexual relationships do not depend on the desire of the one, but of the two together (see 1 Corinthians 7:3–5). In every part of married life, two persons share as equals. But the husband has his place, and the wife has hers. In the family there must be a leader, for the sake of its unity and good running. So the particular duties and responsibilities of wives and husbands are different. The apostle has instructions for both. Let husbands apply their instructions to themselves, rather than see if their wives are applying theirs – and let wives act in the same way.

a. The duties of wives

The wife is called to submit to her husband as leader in the home. They are partners, 'joint heirs of the grace of life' (1 Peter 3:7). They share equally all God's blessings; she is no more the husband's property than he is hers. But when opinions are different in matters concerning the life of the home, the bringing up of the children or anything else, she must respect her husband as the leader and follow his lead. The little phrase 'as to the Lord' in verse 22 means that this is a duty of Christian obedience. 'In everything' in verse 24 may seem difficult, but we should take it to mean that when a woman gives herself to her husband in marriage, her first concern must be for her husband and for her home. This raises many questions today, when women do almost every kind of work that men do, and when many wives spend most of the working day outside the home. Here what is most important is that we do not think what are African or European, American or Asian standards of marriage, but we try to see from the Bible what are Christian standards, and what is God's purpose. So many things that men do, women can do equally well, it is true; but when women marry and are entrusted with children, and then neglect their responsibility of their homes and their children in order to live their own independent lives, the result is sure to be spiritual loss for themselves, their husbands and their children.

b. The duties of husbands

Is the wife's duty to submit to her husband a most difficult one? Could it be more difficult than the standard of love that is required of the husband? Is it hard for the wife to honour and obey her husband? Not if he acts towards her with the self-giving love that these verses describe. Husbands ought to love their wives as themselves, as their own bodies, Paul says in verse 28. Does that not seem very hard? Then work

it out in life. In everything the husband is called to seek
the very highest and best for his wife and never treat
her just as his servant; he is her protector and 'saviour'
(see verse 23). His love must not be only the expression
of his sexual passion, but it must be the Christian love
(for which the Greek New Testament had a different
word) that is completely unselfish. There could not be
a higher standard than verse 25 gives to husbands:
'Husbands, love your wives, as Christ loved the church
and gave himself up for her.' The love of Christ was
perfect, self-giving love – love that at the price of self-
sacrifice sought the cleansing and the purifying of the
church. 'Husbands, love like this', the apostle says.

The husband cannot think, What should my wife do
to be a good wife? He can only think, What must I do
to be a good husband to the one whom God has given
me as my partner? And the wife cannot think, What
can I rightly expect from my husband? She must think,
What is my duty to him, whose life is bound now to
mine?

Prayer. *Almighty God, the Giver of life and all things, in
the wonderful love-union and partnership of marriage Thou
hast bound man and woman together in one. Help husbands
and wives to fulfil the duties, and to find the true blessings and
joys, of Christian marriage, so that in the peace and love and
purity of Christian homes children may be brought up to give
their lives to Thee, for the sake of Jesus Christ our Saviour.*
                                                    AMEN.

Further Study. Study the other passages in the New
Testament which give teaching about the duties of
husbands and wives, and see in what ways they add to
or enlarge on the teaching given here. (1 Corinthians
7:3–5; Colossians 3:18–19; Titus 2:4–5; 1 Peter 3:1–7;
also Matthew 19:3–9; Mark 10:1–12.)

Study 37. CHRIST AND HIS CHURCH

'Wives, be subject to your husbands, as to the Lord. For the husband is the head of the wife as Christ is the head of the church, his body, and is himself its Saviour. As the church is subject to Christ, so let wives also be subject in everything to their husbands. Husbands, love your wives, as Christ loved the church and gave himself up for her, that he might sanctify her, having cleansed her by the washing of water with the word, that he might present the church to himself in splendour, without spot or wrinkle or any such thing, that she might be holy and without blemish. Even so husbands should love their wives as their own bodies. He who loves his wife loves himself. For no man ever hates his own flesh, but nourishes and cherishes it, as Christ does the church, because we are members of his body. "For this reason a man shall leave his father and mother and be joined to his wife, and the two shall become one." This is a great mystery, and I take it to mean Christ and the church; however, let each one of you love his wife as himself, and let the wife see that she respects her husband' (5:22-33).

Paul has taken lessons from the love of Christ for His church to teach husbands their duties to their wives; and from the duties of the church towards Christ, he has taught the duties of wives to their husbands. In this same passage he also argues the other way. There are many names given to the church in the New Testament – the people of God, the household of God, the temple of God, the body of Christ. The church is also called the 'bride of Christ'. Marriage is the closest of all human relationships. There is no closer bond and

union of love than marriage at its highest and best.
There is no more intimate sharing of life. Therefore
marriage can give us a picture, in some ways better
than any other, of the way in which Christ and His
church are bound together in the loving purpose of God.
In verse 31 the apostle quotes what the Old Testament
says (in Genesis 2:24) about God's purpose for marriage:
'For this reason a man shall leave his father and mother
and be joined to his wife, and the two shall become one.'
Then he says that this is to be applied as presenting a
'great mystery', a wonderful revealed truth (see notes
on 1:9 for the word 'mystery'), concerning Christ and
His church. There are three parts of this truth.

a. The love of Christ for His church

There is no human love stronger than the love of man
and woman joined in marriage. A man loves his wife
with a deep and passionate love – it is his nature to love.
Far, far more, and far more perfectly, Christ loves us.
His love is a love that gives and gives and gives. He was
willing to give Himself, even to give His life as a
sacrifice on the cross, for our sakes, that we might be
cleansed, restored, forgiven. Though we are unworthy
of such love, and often unfaithful to it, He loves like
that, and wants to unite us to Himself. In marriage the
union means 'one flesh' – in the church 'he who is
united to the Lord becomes one spirit with him' (1
Corinthians 6:17).

b. The obedience of the church to Christ

In God's pattern and purpose for married life, for the
blessing and harmony of the home, the wife gives herself in loving service, because of the husband who has
given himself to her in devoted love. So the response of

the church as bride of Christ is loyal submission and
loving service. The Christian recognizes the love of
Christ, and the debt owed to Him. The Christian
recognizes the duty of crossing out self-will, and of
acting in obedience to His will in everything. 'I have
been crucified with Christ,' says Paul in Galatians 2:20,
'it is no longer I who live, but Christ who lives in me;
and the life I now live in the flesh I live by faith in the
Son of God, who loved me and gave himself for me.'
That faith, which answers to His love, means dependence on Him and obedience to Him.

c. A bride prepared for her husband

There is a third part to the comparison between the
relationship between husband and wife and the relationship between Christ and His church. We find it in
verses 26 and 27. On her wedding day the bride wants
to appear at her loveliest and her most beautiful for the
man whom she loves. So the purpose of God is that His
church should stand before Him 'in splendour, without
spot or wrinkle or any such thing'. In the first place,
this is only possible by His work. We could never stand
before Him like that through anything that we could do.
We cannot take away the filthy rags of our sins (Isaiah
64:6); only He can take away the evil of our lives and
cleanse us. We cannot of ourselves stand in a wedding
garment that He can accept; we must receive it as His
gift (Matthew 22:11–12). But when He has cleansed us
'by the washing of water' (the outward sign of baptism),
'with the word' (the word that brings the assurance of
His pardon), then we have a duty to keep ourselves
pure. By His strength we must determine to live lives
that are 'holy and without blemish' (verse 27, and see
1:4), lives that are beautiful and lovely in His sight, and
also in the sight of the world.

Prayer. *Lord Jesus, Thou hast loved us with perfect love, giving Thyself for us, even to death; may we give ourselves in loving submission and obedience to Thee, and may we want to live lives that are pure and holy in Thy sight, and in the world may we show forth Thy glory, for Thy name's sake.*

AMEN.

Further Study. 1. Study the Old Testament passages where God is spoken of as the Husband of His people (*e.g.* see Isaiah 54:1–8; 62:4–5; Jeremiah 3:6–14; 31:32; Ezekiel 16 and 23 and Hosea 1–3).

2. Study the use made in the Gospels of marriage celebrations and marriage relationships in our Lord's teaching. (*E.g.* see Matthew 22:1–14; 25:1–13; Mark 2:18–20; John 3:26–30.)

Study 38. PARENTS AND CHILDREN

'Children, obey your parents in the Lord, for this is right. "Honour your father and mother" (this is the first commandment with a promise), "that it may be well with you and that you may live long on the earth." Fathers, do not provoke your children to anger, but bring them up in the discipline and instruction of the Lord' (6:1–4).

Paul has spoken of the duties of wives and husbands, and so he goes on to speak of the duties of children and of parents. For all family relationships are to be made pleasing to God. The home is the first place in which Christian life and duty is to be shown (see Mark 5:18–20 and 1 Timothy 5:4). The witness of a Christian home can speak more for Christ than any other kind of witness.

a. Children

The fifth commandment says 'Honour your father and your mother' (Exodus 20:12). Honour means respect, and speaks of the right attitude of children to their parents. The right attitude must be expressed in the right actions, and this means obeying. Paul adds 'in the Lord'. He may mean, as long as parents do not ask their children to do what would be a denial of their Lord. More likely he means that Christian children's obedience to their parents is their duty to their Lord as well. 'This is right' – there can be no doubt. The commandment of God demands it; the customs of all nations require it. Here is the duty, but there is also encouragement. In the ten commandments, this one has a promise added to it: 'that it may be well with you and that you may live long on the earth.' This does not mean, 'If you obey your parents, you will be sure to live a long life', but, where there is respect and obedience of children for their parents, then that family or tribe or nation will be made strong and enduring – and this cannot be true when family life is weak, when children are rebellious to their parents, and when the home is disordered.

b. Parents

Parents have a solemn duty and responsibility before God. Our children are not our own, to do what we like with them. They are a trust from God. In Exodus 2:9 we read how Pharaoh's daughter said to the mother of Moses, 'Take this child away, and nurse him for me.' The duty of all Christian parents is to care lovingly for their children, to be sure that they grow up strong and well. But it is even more important to see that they grow up to love and serve and obey their Lord. In the New Testament, Timothy provides us with a good example of such growth, nourished by the Word of God, taught and applied by a faithful Christian parent. When we read 2 Timothy 1:5 and 3:14–17, we can see why he grew up to be a man of God. To the Christian parent this spiritual upbringing is more important than any other part of education. For our children to grow up to be godly men and women matters more than that they should be successful or rich or important or clever.

For this reason there must be discipline in the home, but Paul adds a word of warning, when he says, 'do not provoke your children.' It is possible for parents to give unnecessary commands, and to make unnecessary rules. These may provoke, and not lead the children to live a better life. And parents cannot expect obedience from their children unless they are setting them a good example by their own lives. Only then will they lead them to that life 'in the Lord' which should be their highest and greatest desire for them.

Prayer. *Lord God Almighty, the Father of all, bless every Christian home in our land. Give wisdom to parents, that they may bring their children to know and love and serve Thee. And give children the desire to obey, gladly and willingly, and to Thy glory, for Jesus Christ's sake.* AMEN.

Note. Verse 2 speaks of the fifth commandment as 'the first commandment' or 'a first commandment' with a promise. It may be right to take these words to mean that the commandment is one of primary importance (as Matthew 23:23 and Mark 12:28 speak of commandments of greater and lesser importance). Or it may mean the first commandment that is learnt by children. Or it may mean the first of the ten to have a promise – we would then have to understand the words at the end of the second commandment simply as a statement of the grace of God.

Further Study. 1. Study other passages in the Bible
that speak of the duties of children to their parents.
See Exodus 20:12; Deuteronomy 5:16; Matthew 15:3–6;
Colossians 3:20; 1 Timothy 5:4, 8.

2. Study also Bible passages that speak of the
responsibilities of parents. *E.g.* see Deuteronomy 4:9;
6:4–7; 11:18–19; Proverbs 12:6 and Colossians 3:21.

Study 39. SERVANTS AND MASTERS

'Slaves, be obedient to those who are your earthly
masters, with fear and trembling, in singleness
of heart, as to Christ; not in the way of eye-
service, as men-pleasers, but as servants of
Christ, doing the will of God from the heart,
rendering service with a good will as to the Lord
and not to men, knowing that whatever good any
one does, he will receive the same again from the
Lord, whether he is a slave or free. Masters, do
the same to them, and forbear threatening,
knowing that he who is both their Master and
yours is in heaven, and that there is no partiality
with him' (6:5–9).

At the time in which the New Testament was
written there were large numbers of slaves, who served
in the homes or on the farms of those who owned them.
Many of these slaves had become Christians, and Paul
wrote to them about their duties. We are thankful
that – largely through the influence of Christianity –
slavery has been abolished in most countries in the
world. Nevertheless what the apostle says here can
apply to the duties of servants and masters today, in
the home or anywhere else. There are principles in
these verses that should still guide Christian employees
and employers.

a. The duties of servants

We may sum up what verses 5–8 say about the duties of servants, under four headings.

1. The duty of obedience. We have a duty to serve and to obey those who are set over us. They are our 'earthly masters'. We serve them with the thought of our heavenly Master always in mind. We honour Him by faithful service (see Titus 2:9–10), and never by rebelling against what we are asked to do.

2. Singleness of heart. There is no place for half-hearted service in the Christian's life; nothing but the best that he can do is good enough.

3. Service as to Christ. All that the Christian does, he should do as for Christ Himself (see Romans 14:7–9). He may feel that his earthly master does not deserve his best work. He should still do it in order to honour Christ. He should feel that 'every single piece of work he produces must be good enough to show to God' (Barclay). This is a very high standard. It means also that he is not just a 'men-pleaser'. In some businesses you can always tell whether the manager is in or out, by the way that the employees are working. Many people speak and act in one way when their master is present, and in another way when he is absent. For the Christian such double standards are impossible. In all things he is to 'do the will of God', do it 'as to Christ', and do it 'from the heart'.

4. For the sake of the Lord's reward. In some cases, however hard the Christian servant works, his master never gives him credit, but is still cruel and unjust. The Christian slave in New Testament days often found this. He was not to worry. There may be misunderstanding and no just reward here. God has seen, and His word is, 'whatever good any one does, he will receive the same again from the Lord.' Nothing that is done for Him is

ever done in vain (see 1 Corinthians 15:58; Colossians
3:24–25). He will bring every single work of ours into
judgment. Nothing will be hidden in the coming day
of the Lord (Matthew 10:26; 2 Corinthians 5:10). For
every evil thing, for every failure of our lives, we need
His grace and forgiveness; every good thing He has
seen and will remember, even if in this life it has
brought only evil on our heads. The Christian, in all
his life and work and relationships, lives with Christ as
Master, Witness and Judge.

b. The duties of masters

Servants have challenging instructions to apply to
themselves, but so do masters, and all those who have
authority over others. 'Do the same', Paul says to them.
He must mean, 'act in the same kind of way' – 'as to
Christ', doing what is right in God's sight, whatever
other men may do. If we have people under us, we are
to act with 'good will' towards them, 'doing the will of
God' and what is right in His sight, and doing it 'from
the heart'. There is to be no 'threatening', no cruelty or
injustice in word or in action. We are not to take
advantage of our position or our authority over others.
Above all there is this reminder, 'You have a Master in
heaven. On earth there may be none who will call
you to account. There is One to whom you must give
account in heaven; you cannot escape Him, and He
sees and knows all that you do.' Moreover 'there is no
partiality with him'. In the world we see rich and poor,
master and servant, some with great power and
authority, and others with none. Before God all of these
are equal (Galatians 3:28). In the day of His judgment
this will become perfectly clear. In our Lord's parable
(Luke 16:19–31) the rich man and Lazarus were of
equal importance in God's sight, though they were not

so in man's sight. 'It is appointed for men to die once, and after that comes judgment' (Hebrews 9:27). This is a particular truth that Paul would remind masters and those in positions of great authority to apply to themselves.

Prayer. *Lord, God Almighty, King of kings, and Lord of all men, when we have authority over others, help us to act in humility, in love and kindness, knowing that we are Thy servants. When we serve others, help us to do so as in Thy sight, and to Thy glory in all things, for the sake of Jesus Christ our Master.* AMEN.

Note. In his Epistles Paul did not write about slavery as an institution. In writing to Philemon about his runaway slave Onesimus, he suggests that he should receive him back no longer as a slave, but as a brother (Philemon 16). He never urged slaves to rebel against their masters. Christianity would have soon begun to appear as a programme for social reform if he had done this. He emphasizes spiritual things first. The most important thing that Christian slaves had to do was to glorify Christ in their work and in their lives. It was for Christian masters to see the full meaning of Christian teaching, and to decide to put slavery to an end; and in the fullness of time this is what happened.

Further Study. 1. Study the teaching of other passages in the New Testament, addressed like this to 'slaves', such as Colossians 3:22–25; 1 Timothy 6:1–2; Titus 2:9–10 and 1 Peter 2:18–25.

2. What principles can be applied to our own situation from the Old Testament instructions to those who had servants or slaves under them? *e.g.* in Deuteronomy 5:14–15; 15:1–6, 12–18 and 16:11–12.

6:10–20. THE CHRISTIAN CONFLICT

In what has gone before in this letter, Paul has written about the great privileges and blessings that the Christian has in Christ. He has written about the kind of life to which he is called, personally and in the fellowship of the Christian church. He has written about the way that Christians should act in their relationships towards others, especially towards those closest to them – husbands and wives, parents and children, servants and masters. None of these things is easy. The Christian life cannot be lived without facing great difficulties and opposition. From beginning to end it is conflict, and before the apostle closes this letter he wants to remind his readers about this Christian warfare, about the power of the enemy, about the greater power of our Captain, and about the armour that the Christian needs.

Study 40. STRENGTH FOR BATTLE

'Finally, be strong in the Lord and in the strength of his might. Put on the whole armour of God, that you may be able to stand against the wiles of the devil. For we are not contending against flesh and blood, but against the principalities, against the powers, against the world rulers of this present darkness, against the spiritual hosts of wickedness in the heavenly places' (6:10–12).

No army should go out to battle without thinking both about the strength they have, and about the power of the enemy they have to fight against. The soldiers in Christ's army must do the same (see Luke 14:31–33).

a. The power of the enemy

The Christian needs to realize the powers of evil against which he has to fight. Firstly, they are spiritual powers 'in the heavenly places'; the powers of evil are not flesh and blood – that is, they are human – though they work through men. Spiritual powers can be met and conquered only by the spiritual power of God. Secondly, they are powers that have come to control the world (see John 12:31), and try to hold the people of the world in the darkness of wickedness. They must be resisted, lest we as 'children of light' (5:8), 'delivered . . . from the dominion of darkness' (Colossians 1:13), are brought back into darkness. Thirdly, it is not only power we have to face, but cleverness and deceit – 'the wiles of the devil' (see again 4:14, and 2 Corinthians 2:11). Sometimes it seems that the devil uses every cunning method possible to turn us away from our Master to do what is evil.

b. The power of our Captain

The power of our enemy is strong, but we can be sure that the power of the Lord whom we serve is stronger. He has conquered all the powers of evil (Colossians 2:15). We cannot be strong in our own strength. 'Apart from me you can do nothing' Jesus has said (John 15:5). The true meaning of the words in verse 10 here is not so much 'be strong' as 'be strengthened'. In other words, 'receive His strength, and then you will be strong'; and as in 1:19 Paul uses here three different words to speak of that power that we can have, if we are living 'in the Lord' (see again also the prayer of 3:16). 'He who is in you is greater than he who is in the world' (1 John 4:4). So through Christ we can be 'more than conquerors' (Romans 8:37).

> Be valiant, be strong,
> Resist the power of sin.
> The fight is long, the foe is strong,
> But you shall win.
> For through the power of Christ,
> The stronger than the strong,
> You shall be more than conquerors –
> Be valiant, be strong.

In many ways the New Testament speaks of the Christian life as warfare. (See references under 'Further Study' below.) Here the apostle's emphasis is on the personal nature of the conflict. We are all in the battle, all who are Christ's men and women. We must fight together; but there are many battles that (humanly speaking) we have to fight alone. They are like the wrestling of one man against another. That is the battle which Paul has specially in mind here. It is indeed true that often the Christian goes out to do battle for his Master; he must conquer the powers of evil in order to bring others into the kingdom of Jesus Christ. At other times, however, the Christian has to defend himself, to be sure that he is not driven back, back into evil, back into the darkness. So Paul says four times in verses 11–14, 'stand . . . withstand . . . stand . . . stand', and he speaks of the armour that protects the Christian soldier, and makes him able to stand (verse 11). In our next study we will consider that armour.

Prayer. *Lord Jesus Christ, the Captain of our salvation,* *help us to know our own weakness, but much more help us to know Thy strength; may we realize the power of the evil one, but much more may we realize Thy power; so that, strong in Thee, we may stand firm for all that is true and right and good and lovely, and may glorify Thy name in the world, now and always.* AMEN.

Further Study. Make a study of the different ways in which the New Testament speaks of the Christian life as warfare. Look up the following references, but add others to the list: 1 Corinthians 9:26-27; 2 Corinthians 10:3-5; 1 Thessalonians 5:8; 1 Timothy 1:18; 6:12; 2 Timothy 2:3-4; 4:7; James 4:7; 1 Peter 5:8-9; Revelation 12:7-11.

Study 41. THE CHRISTIAN'S ARMOUR

'Therefore take the whole armour of God, that you may be able to withstand in the evil day, and having done all, to stand. Stand therefore, having girded your loins with truth, and having put on the breastplate of righteousness, and having shod your feet with the equipment of the gospel of peace; above all taking the shield of faith, with which you can quench all the flaming darts of the evil one. And take the helmet of salvation, and the sword of the Spirit, which is the word of God' (6:13-17).

While Paul wrote this letter, he was 'in chains' (verse 20). Probably he was living in a hired house in Rome, but as a Roman prisoner, chained night and day to a Roman soldier (see Acts 28:16,20). He would often think of the armour that the Roman soldier had to wear, and so of the spiritual armour that the soldier of

Christ must wear, if he is to win his battle, and be able
'in the evil day' (when trial and temptation are their
most powerful) 'to stand'. The Christian soldier needs
'the whole armour', each part of which Paul now
describes.

a. The girdle of truth

Then, as in many parts of Asia and Africa today, men
wore long flowing garments. If a man wanted to move
quickly or work seriously, those garments had to be
tied round with a girdle. Before the soldier put on his
armour, he had to put the girdle round his garments
that were under the armour. 'Truth' is the Christian's
girdle. God wants in the Christian's life 'truth in the
inward being' (Psalm 51:6). Unless there is truth and
sincerity and honesty in our lives, we cannot be ready
to work for Christ, or to do battle for God. In Isaiah
11:5 truth is described as Messiah's girdle. It must be
the girdle of His disciples too.

b. The breastplate of righteousness

The breastplate protects the heart, and no soldier in
those days would go to fight without one. Righteousness
is the Christian's breastplate. It is difficult to be quite
sure what Paul means here, because righteousness is
used in two different ways in the New Testament.
There is God's righteousness, which is His gift to us;
when we trust Him, we have forgiveness of our sin, and
the gift of His righteousness and His salvation. Here
(since later Paul speaks of 'the helmet of salvation'), he
may mean the right actions which are the result of God's
grace and working in our lives. Then it is a matter of
doing what is right, doing the will of God – and
certainly it is only when we want righteousness in this

way that we can possibly have victory in the Christian life. ('Righteousness' in this sense is spoken of in 5:9 and also in Romans 14:17.)

c. Shod with the gospel of peace

Many people have taken this to mean that the Christian soldier is also the messenger of the gospel, and the sandals of the Christian speak of his readiness to go out with the gospel. We have seen, however, that Paul's main thought in these verses is of the ability of the soldier to stand firm against the enemy. The Roman soldier wore boots with strong nails that gave him a firm foothold in the battle. The Christian can stand firm in the battle only as he knows very surely the peace with God that comes to us only through the gospel of Jesus Christ. Without that peace, which gives the certainty of God's presence and blessing, a person is anxious and 'in the evil day' will fall.

d. The shield of faith

In warfare in Paul's day they often put the darts or arrows in tar, lit them, and then sent them burning against their enemy. Sometimes the temptations of the evil one come against us like 'flaming darts'. There is only one way to stop them. The soldier had a great wooden shield covered with leather, to stop the darts and to stop them burning. Faith is the Christian's shield. Trusting in the power and protection of God, the Christian can turn back every temptation. He has no other way.

e. The helmet of salvation

The head needs special protection. To be wounded

there means death. The salvation of God means life for the Christian; by it he is saved from spiritual death. And this, like every other piece of the armour, the Christian receives from his Captain's hand. He must accept it as His gift. He could not make such a helmet for himself.

f. The sword of the Spirit

Lastly, Paul names the Christian's sword, 'the word of God'. This is the Christian's weapon as he goes out to do battle for his Lord. It is the Christian's weapon as he defends himself. The Lord Himself used this weapon in His temptations. 'It is written', He said time after time (see Matthew 4:4,7,10). How can we know, when 'the wiles of the devil' are so deceitful, what is right, and what is a temptation to do wrong? We can know only as we learn and use the word which God has spoken, showing us the right. The word, given by the Spirit, is our sword. 'How can a young man keep his way pure?' said the psalmist. 'By guarding it according to thy word' (Psalm 119:9).

Prayer. *O Lord our God, we thank Thee for all that is provided for us. May we not fail to accept from Thy hand the armour we need. Help us to put on each piece with prayer. So, in the battle, may we not stumble, nor fall back, nor bring shame and defeat to Thy cause, for Thy great name's sake.* AMEN.

Further Study. With these verses consider other passages which speak of the 'armour of God': Isaiah 59:16–17, where the Lord Himself is the Warrior; Isaiah 11:4–5; 2 Corinthians 6:7; and 1 Thessalonians 5:8, where the detail is different, but the essential meaning is similar.

Study 42. VICTORY THROUGH PRAYER

'Pray at all times in the Spirit, with all prayer and supplication. To that end keep alert with all perseverance, making supplication for all the saints, and also for me, that utterance may be given me in opening my mouth boldly to proclaim the mystery of the gospel, for which I am an ambassador in chains; that I may declare it boldly, as I ought to speak' (6:18-20).

Prayer is not exactly a part of the Christian's armour, but it is connected very closely with it. How can the Christian 'be strong in the Lord' (verse 10)? By putting on each piece of the armour, and by prayer. Prayer is the way of victory, because prayer connects the Christian with his unconquerable Lord. So the hymn rightly says, 'Satan trembles, when he sees the weakest saint upon his knees.' Paul has much to say in these verses about the Christian's prayer life, and then he has a special request for the prayers of his readers for himself.

a. Real prayer

Paul uses two different words for prayer here (there are four set together in Philippians 4:6 and 1 Timothy 2:1). One speaks of the general dependence on God in prayer, the other of special requests. There are many different kinds of prayer and ways of prayer. And prayer is to be made 'at all times'. Every time is the right time for prayer; every event in life should be marked by prayer (see Romans 12:12; Colossians 4:2; 1 Thessalonians 5:17). This is easy to say and to accept, but hard to do. We have to 'keep alert', alert that other things do not take the time that we should give to prayer. It needs 'all perseverance', because whenever we turn to pray so many other thoughts flood into our minds to hinder prayer, and there are so many difficulties. We have to persevere, but not just in our own strength. God gives us His Spirit in our hearts, to help us to pray, to guide us and make us strong to continue in prayer. (See Romans 8:26–27.) When our life is 'in Christ', 'in the Spirit', united to our Lord, He gives all the grace and help that we need for prayer.

Then it is wonderful to realize that this prayer can be offered 'for all the saints'. There are none beyond the reach of prayer. We may not be able to help our leaders in their responsibilities by any other means; we help them in their work when we pray for them. We can pray for our loved ones, for those whom we have been able to help along the way of Christ, for those who are thousands of miles away, for those who live in places where the church is persecuted. We can pray for all of them, and our God is a God who unfailingly answers prayer.

b. A special request for prayer

Pray 'for all the saints', the apostle says, but he also asks prayer for himself. He prays for these Christians to whom he is writing (see 1:15–23; 3:14–21), but he wants their prayers for him too. Prayer makes us all equal before God. The fervent prayer of an apostle is not worth more to God than the sincere petition of the simplest child of God. So the apostle not only says to the churches, 'I am praying for you', but he asks the churches to pray for him (see Colossians 4:3; 1 Thessalonians 5:25; 2 Thessalonians 3:1). The churches needed prayer; their apostle needed prayer. He was 'in chains' for Christ's sake. He faced special temptations where he was. He needed grace every day, given in answer to prayer. Two things he needed more than anything else. First, he was still 'an ambassador'. He still had opportunities to represent Christ and to set forward His kingdom. So he still needed wisdom and guidance 'in opening his mouth'. He needed to be given the right words to speak, that would turn the hearers towards Christ. (Compare the prayer of Psalm 51:15.) Secondly, he needed boldness. Every Christian – even an apostle – often faces the temptation to say what people want to hear rather than what God wants them to hear. Those who realize this, and who know the temptation to put the praise of men above the praise of God, want to make this prayer for themselves, and want others to make it for them in their witness to the gospel – that 'I may declare it boldly, as I ought to speak'.

Prayer. *Lord God Almighty, we praise Thee that we can come to Thee in prayer. We ask Thee to give us opportunities to speak for Thee. Give us words to speak, and courage at all times. Help us also to be faithful and persevering in prayer for all whose needs we know; and knowing Thy abundant answers to prayer, may we praise Thee for ever and ever, through Jesus Christ our Saviour.* AMEN.

Further Study. 1. Consider other New Testament passages where the duty of alertness or watchfulness is set forward, and consider especially its connection with prayer. See Mark 13:33; 14:34–38; Luke 21:36; 1 Corinthians 16:13; 1 Thessalonians 5:6; 1 Peter 4:7; Revelation 3:2–3 and 16:15.

2. Study how the New Testament in other places speaks of the 'boldness' of Christians, and how prayer is made for 'boldness'. See especially Acts 4:13, 29, 31 and Philippians 1:20.

6:21–24. CONCLUSION

Study 43. A FINAL MESSAGE AND GREETING

'Now that you also may know how I am and what
I am doing, Tychicus the beloved brother and
faithful minister in the Lord will tell you everything. I have sent him to you for this very purpose,
that you may know how we are, and that he may
encourage your hearts.
Peace be to the brethren, and love with faith,
from God the Father and the Lord Jesus Christ.
Grace be with all who love our Lord Jesus Christ
with love undying' (6:21–24).

Here are the last words of Paul to his readers, telling
how they will gain personal news of him, bringing his
prayer and greeting, and with them a challenge.

a. Personal news

All through this letter Paul has said nothing of himself, except that he is the Lord's 'ambassador in chains'
(verse 20), a 'prisoner for the Lord' (4:1). All through
the letter he has named no individual, until he names
Tychicus here. The purpose of the letter has been to
tell from beginning to end of the glory of Christ, and
the greatness of His purpose for His church – so much so
that the apostle feels that it has not been the place to
speak about himself. Yet he knows that many friends
who read the letter would be anxious for him (see 3:13),
and he wants them to be comforted by good news of
him in prison (compare Philippians 1:12–20). So he

tells them that Tychicus, who brings this letter (and also Colossians and Philemon), will give them the news they want to hear. He says two things about Tychicus. He was a 'beloved brother' to Paul, and he was a 'faithful minister', serving the Lord. He was, in short, one of those quietly faithful men by whom the church in any generation lives and grows (see 2 Timothy 2:2).

b. A prayer

The letter began with that regular greeting of the apostle, which is more a prayer than a social greeting, 'Grace to you and peace from God our Father and the Lord Jesus Christ' (1:2). It ends with that same prayer for peace in the hearts of 'the brethren', the peace with God and with one another about which Paul has said so much, especially in chapter 2. Not only does he pray for 'peace' (their well-being as individuals and in the fellowship), but also for 'love with faith'. In one way love follows faith. Love comes into the heart of those who are united by faith to Christ. But 'faith' in the New Testament sometimes means 'faithfulness' and not just 'trust'. He prays that they may have that love which he has said in 1 Corinthians 13:7 'bears all things, believes all things, hopes all things, endures all things'. Then his last petition in his prayer is like the first – for 'grace'. Grace includes everything else, because God's grace to us is His attitude of love and mercy, which makes Him want to give us every single thing that we need. Without His grace, every moment and every hour, we have nothing, and we are nothing. With His grace we have all we need, and we are nothing less than sons of God.

c. A challenge

To whom does God offer His grace? To all, but the ones who receive it most are those most conscious of their need; and they, knowing and accepting it, are full of praise for the Lord, who is the Giver of all grace. And those who are full of praise will also be full of love for the Lord Jesus Christ, because of all that He is, and all that He has done. So Paul says, 'Grace be with all who love our Lord Jesus Christ', and then adds, 'with love undying'. The last word that he uses can have two meanings. The older versions translated it as 'in un-corruptness'. It may mean that which is morally un-corrupt, that which is pure and completely sincere. At least that is a challenge to us – our love is to be like that, absolutely sincere, devoted entirely to Him who has loved us enough to die for us. Then secondly, the word means 'immortal' or 'undying'. The love of God for us is an eternal love. That eternal love must be in our hearts, love that will not fail and will not die away. The love of the world may tempt us, but it must not move us from our love for Him. Real love never fails, 'never ends', though everything else may change or fail (1 Corinthians 13:8). Love is the greatest thing. For love, based on thankfulness for His grace, leads us to worship, witness, serve and obey Him; and in the end love will lead us to see His face, and be satisfied for ever.

Prayer. *Lord of all love and grace, fill our hearts with faith, with thankfulness, and with love that will shine more and more brightly to the perfect day.* AMEN.

Further Study. 1. From the study of verses 21–22, with Colossians 4:7–9 and Philemon 9–10, what evidence is there that the three letters were written at the same time and sent by the same messenger?

2. In Romans 2:7, 2 Timothy 1:10, and 1 Peter 3:4 the same original word is used as that translated 'undying' here. How do these references help to explain the word in this verse?